YOU ARE WORTH WHATEVER YOU ARE PAID

I left the government in late 1980 and started a consulting firm. I decided that I would charge a daily consulting fee 50 percent above the maximum paid to individual consultants by federal agencies. That came out to something more than $250 a day, and for six months I charged that amount. About mid-1981 I was approached by a representative of a Fortune 100 company and was asked to make a one-day presentation. I agreed, and when asked for my per diem fee, I blurted out, "$950." I don't know why I picked that number. Maybe the devil made me do it. In any case, the customer didn't blink. He didn't have me arrested. He didn't threaten my wife and family. He said, "Okay." I was stunned, but quickly added, "Plus expenses, of course . . ."

WORKING ALONE

MURRAY FELSHER, Ph.D.

BERKLEY BOOKS, NEW YORK

WORKING ALONE

A Berkley Book / published by arrangement with
the author

PRINTING HISTORY
Berkley trade paperback edition / September 1994

ISBN: 0-425-15824-1

BERKLEY®
Berkley Books are published by The Berkley Publishing Group,
200 Madison Avenue, New York, New York 10016.
BERKLEY and the "B" design
are trademarks belonging to Berkley Publishing Corporation.

PRINTED IN THE UNITED STATES OF AMERICA

10   9   8   7   6   5   4   3   2   1

To my family

To my wife, Natalie
To my daughter, Elyann
To my sons Harry and Joshua
         the four reasons I do what I do

To work alone and to succeed at it
requires the abiding love and support of
a family

CONTENTS

PREFACE

Salaried employees of large institutions have always shared a singular dream—that of running their own businesses, being their own bosses, and generally having total control of their working environs. A significant number of these individuals have also sought the very special rewards to be gleaned by actually working alone, where they are beholden to none and are wholly responsible for their own economic well-being.

In the strange times in which we now find ourselves, the once-esoteric phrases as "institutional downsizing," "corporate restructuring," and "administrative layoffs" are now commonplace; everyone from the hourly employee to the profit-sharing executive finds himself in harm's way—one or two paychecks away from economic disaster. In these times more and more people—by choice, by chance, or by pink slip—are finding themselves "on the street," and more and more of these same people are choosing to work alone.

Working Alone is primarily addressed to these people and to those who will find themselves in similar circumstances. Much of the book can also be applied to owners of small businesses, as the circumstances of the small business owner are indeed similar to, if not actually congruent with, an individual working alone. The book is not a how-to manual, but instead is geared to establishing a certain frame of mind in the reader, a frame of mind necessary for success in this daring venture of "going it alone." *Working Alone* presents sixty-seven short pieces, written in a personal, informal tone. Each is constructed with a specific point in mind; the objective of the whole is to increase the reader's level of confidence and self-esteem and to create a mind-set that will allow him to not only function well, but to also win the end game associated with working alone—which translates as continued monetary success.

INTRODUCTION

Many years ago, in a galaxy far, far away, when our oldest child was entering college, our savings were at their lowest and our debts were at their highest, I quit my job at National Aeronautics and Space Administration headquarters in Washington, D.C. On October 3, 1980 I was earning the maximum salary paid to a civil servant; on October 4, 1980 I brought home "zero." No pension, no medical benefits, nothing. (My rationale, such as it was, was published as a poem in *Co-Evolution Quarterly*—copy on request.)

Still, I gave myself two years to make a go of it outside the fuzzy warmth of government employ, and held out to myself the option of returning to the federal bureaucracy should I not be able to earn an honest living otherwise.

Well, it's been well more than a decade now. I publish three newsletters and am a successful consultant. I have no intention of rejoining the government. This is not so unusual a tale in this odd capital city of ours. What *is* unusual and what forms the basis of the book you are about to read, is that I have done this—and am still doing this— *alone*. That's right, alone. No secretary, no receptionist, no staff, no accountant, no bookkeeper, no lawyer, no business manager—no one.

I mean this book to have practical value in an offbeat sense. To that end it is comprised of short, deliberate, and topical essays, each meant to point out a specific technique, method, hazard, opinion, or bias. Tucked in, here and there, I have inserted particular notions that will serve as lane markers, defining a philosophical outlook I have used as a guide these past years. Perhaps it would also be as important to point out what this book is *not:* (1) It is not a step-by-step, how-you-can-get-into-the-business manual; (2) It is not a handbook informing you how to best fill out IRS Schedules C, SE, etc; and (3) It is not a pump-'em-up, watch-'em-go sales seminar.

My goal is to be entertainingly practical and thoughtfully pragmatic. By example, and in a rather personal manner, I hope to show you how to create for yourself a mind-set conducive to an end game similar to the one that I am now playing, winning, and most important, enjoying.

Happy reading!

—M. Felsher,
Washington D.C., May 1994

1 WORKING ALONE DOES NOT MEAN BEING A LONER

Working alone makes it necessary to establish, cultivate, and ever-expand your circle of contacts and your knowledge/information base

Working alone does not necessarily mean that you must establish yourself as a "loner." In fact, to do so would significantly diminish your options as to the possibilities of acquiring work for yourself. Even if you have inherited a set of selfish genes and truly dislike working with or doing favors for other people, remember that a favor granted places the grantee in debt to you. He will know that to receive another favor from you he must first return one in kind. Akin to "I'll scratch your back, you scratch mine," this method of mutual manipulation will quickly establish for you a substantial interactive network. As an example; this morning I received a call from a congressional staff member who needed some information, which I provided. Without prodding on my part, he volunteered the (as yet unpublished) date of a hearing his committee is to hold, related to a subject he knew I was following. And so it goes.

The accumulation of knowledge for its own sake is considered in some quarters to be a scholarly and fulfilling occupation. In truth, it is nothing more than shallow and self-gratifying. Our civilization moves forward by integrating the continual flux of social and physical interaction. By accepting, accumulating, and *not* passing on knowledge, you perpetrate a social disservice—in fact, the more you know and keep closely hidden, the less you are able to financially gain from that knowledge.

1

Working alone then, means that it is all the more necessary to keep in close touch with all that is happening around you. The effort that you will have to expend is pro-active; that is, there is no daily coffee klatch, no proximal nucleus of peers to whom you can passively attune. It will require significant effort on your part—and even with that effort, I cannot guarantee your ultimate success. But without that effort, I *can* guarantee your ultimate failure.

2 GOING FOR THE GOLD

Use all opportunities available to you to make money—like writing a book

Don't be bashful about making money. After all, nearly everyone you know has got a salaried job. This means that after a week or two, or maybe a month, that person gets an envelope with a check in it placed in his hand. And he gets it every payday, regularly, on schedule. Some people you know work hard for their salaries, some work very little, and some work not at all. But when you work alone, nobody comes up to you and places a check in your hands on a regular basis. No way. That's why you headed off on your own, right? But that means you must look for every opportunity to make a buck. It is not gross. It is not tacky. What you bring in will be proportional solely to your own abilities and talents, and will vary, over time, according to those same characteristics. No one will pay you if you do not come forth with the product or service you promised. And the more things you are able to do, the more money you will be able to generate. As an example, I give you the book you are now reading. You paid good money for it. I hope it is doing you some good—I know it's doing me *much* good.

3 | WHAT "THEY" WILL THINK IS NONE OF YOUR CONCERN

Be responsible only to yourself. Don't worry about satisfying someone else's expectations

"What will they think?" Talk about a bucketful of ice water. What will they think? Those are the four most detrimental words that can be uttered by a person considering working alone. After all, you have no one to lord it over, no one to stand over and proclaim, "See, I'm giving you orders, and that makes me much better than you. I occupy a much higher organization stratum." Hey, working alone, you don't even *have* an organization. Undoubtedly, there will be those among your family and friends who will gaze down their collective noses at anyone to whom nobody reports. Bad mistake on their part. Next time they pass a comment in this regard, remind them that if no one reports to you, then you also report to no one. And be certain to remind them of that again, in a not too kindly fashion, when they come storming in to let off steam because their boss chewed them out for some infraction or another. Being responsible, in a business sense, only to yourself means that you don't have to protect yourself from a subordinate's schemes or a supervisor's dreams (or vice versa). All you've got to do is advance yourself for your own self's sake, and if someone has a problem with that, let them work it out on their own time.

4

SEPARATING THE PAYER FROM THE PARASITE

Getting 'em to sign on the bottom line

We all like to get information free. And there are times you may decide to forgo immediate payment for services rendered in favor of a possible future payoff. But suppose you are approached—in person, by mail, by fax, or by phone—by someone who wants information but does not indicate if, or how, he will hire you to pay for that information. Well, lucky you. You are about to memorize a question that, admittedly, I was *not* clever enough to ask when I first started out (and thereby hang one or two sad tales to be told in later pages). Suffice it to say that, once having ascertained that your "customer" is to be charged for the information you will impart to him, ask thusly: *"How do we arrange the billing for my services?"* Unless and until a written contract is negotiated and executed you would do well to discuss any matter except the one for which he has to pay you. Memorize that question, and have no qualms about using it early on in your initial discussions. You will very quickly learn whether you are dealing with a serious client or a frivolous brain sucker. Cultivate the former, and avoid the latter like the plague.

5 YOU ARE WORTH WHATEVER YOU ARE PAID

Ask not and you will get not

In our free enterprise society, we place monetary values upon an individual's time spent and effort expended. These monetary values are called salaries, commissions, fees, etc. In the federal establishment, there is a pay scale called a GS schedule, with fifteen GS grades, each with ten in-grade steps, followed by a Senior Executive Service (SES) schedule. Working alone, one does not have the luxury of establishing a remuneration schedule to match this rigid register. Instead, one must establish a facile scale commensurate with the service being offered. Too often, especially when a person starts out working alone, he becomes very grateful to his initial customers and responds by charging them far too little for his services rendered. As difficult as this is to believe, please take the following on faith: *Your customer will rather pay more than less for your services.*

As a consultant in my own technical field, my fees go from zero (yes, zero, and we'll talk about that later) to more than $5,000 per day. The rate is related directly to (a) the affluence of the customer, (b) the immediacy of his need, (c) the ability of anybody else to fulfill that need, and (d) the degree of greed that happens to infect me on that particular day. (These in no particular order.) As to engagements as an after-dinner speaker and the like, the sky's the limit.

The customer will expect to pay the maximum for the service you are rendering to him. Indeed, if he could perform that service himself, or if he could have one of his salaried

6

employees perform that service, he would surely have done so. The fact that you are being asked to provide him with this service is proof enough that he is willing to pay, and pay well. If you, for any reason, were to now lowball your fee, you would plant in his mind a viable seed of doubt as to your own credibility. "After all," the customer would think, "If this guy were really any good, I would be paying twice what he is asking." And there goes your future with that customer.

Your worth increases with your fee. Example: I left the government in late 1980 and started a consulting firm. (It's called Associated Technical Consultants. More about ATC later.) I decided that I would charge a daily consulting fee 50 percent above the maximum paid to individual consultants by federal agencies. That came out to something more than $250 a day, and for six months I charged that amount. About mid-1981, I was approached by a representative of a Fortune-One Hundred company and was asked to make a one-day presentation. I agreed, and when asked for my per diem fee, I blurted out, "$950." I don't know why I picked that number. Maybe the devil made me do it. In any case, the customer didn't blink. He didn't have me arrested. He didn't threaten my wife and family. He said, "Okay." I was stunned, but quickly added, "Plus expenses, of course." And thereby I learned a major, major lesson. Always ask for more. The money is not coming out of the personal pocket of the customer. If he gets what he wants, in terms of information, then it is worth far more to him than the few extra dollars you had asked for. And if you do charge the higher rate, then surely you must be worth it. Finally, by establishing a high rate to begin with, a long-term relationship will then provide the time to extend your rates even higher as the years go by. In June 1991, I was asked to provide a half-day briefing to management of this same company and charged $5,000. I wasn't embarrassed asking that amount, and they weren't reluctant to pay it.

6 | ALWAYS CARRY YOUR RESUME*

Know thyself, and let all know thee as well

Because of chance encounters and other unplanned events, I've had occasion to hand someone my resume: on an airplane, at a Jiffy-Lube, on an escalator, on an elevator, over lunch, on a subway, on a park bench (yes, even there). Mind you, I do not tap strangers on the shoulder and, unsolicited, jam my resume under their armpits. The above chance meetings led to brief discussions, and often to a realization (by the other party) that there might be a reason to learn something more about what consulting services I might offer. At that point, out comes a single-page resume, unashamedly proffered, and (usually) gratefully accepted, in exchange for the other's business card. I should immediately point out that the one-pager is really a tease, and is meant to elicit a response within a few working days. If no response is forthcoming by that time, then a follow-up telephone call is in order. In any case, I then send my biographical sketch. It runs to six pages—altogether too long according to some, but just right according to me. If the one-pager has long since been resting at either the bottom of the "round file" or some bird cage, then the six-pager will no doubt realize the same fate. However, if the one-pager has whetted the

---

*Except maybe when you're in the shower. And by the way, I do not make a point of noting that you should always carry your business card—that goes without saying.

appetite of the potential customer, then the six-pager will do much to satisfy him. In either case, the time and effort involved are minimal and well worth it.

Your resume and biographical sketch should be continuously updated. I keep a folder next to my computer and drop in slips of paper which get entered into the hard disk every other week.

7 | NEVER BE ASHAMED OF MAKING MONEY

Somebody has to pay the bills, and it might as well be you

There is something that lives in our collective heads that produces pangs of embarrassment when we are caught in the honest pursuit of making money. Somehow, the actual effort to make money is considered in some quarters as crass. However, many of these same people consider the *spending* of money as awfully necessary, if not obligatory.

Indeed, it is our own ability to make money that translates, through our taxes and contributions, to the whole spectrum of activities we call our "way of life." My approach is relatively simple (and perhaps simpleminded, as well). You see, I believe that as an individual, you should engage in sufficient activities that result in the most payback for the least effort in the shortest time. Almost tautological, this philosophy will nonetheless take many people by surprise. There are those we all know who will work the longest hours and expend the most energy to receive the least payback. These people are called "martyrs," and when you are working alone, you can never, ever, don the cloak of the martyr. At best you can approach a martyr with your one-page resume and offer him your services as a management consultant.

8 | WHAT INFORMATION DO YOU GIVE AWAY FREE?

To freebie or not to freebie, that is the question

How much information do you give away free? As the only participating member of my enterprising empire, my organization can do only one thing at a time. So what do I do if someone calls and wants my time, but doesn't intend paying for it. For every hour I give something away free, I lose an hour's worth of some money-making activity. Does that mean that one should never do anything for free? Nope. In fact, some of the more lucrative assignments I've had, have had their origins in a bit of work performed at no charge. Scatter your freebies wisely and they will come back to reward you.

Two rules to follow:

(1) Always spend time with students writing theses and dissertations. Your background and experience are negotiable currency with these individuals. They will cite you in their bibliographies and quote you in their presentations at national meetings. There is no way of knowing how many hundreds of people now have knowledge of you, people who would otherwise not have known of your work. Further, these graduate students eventually receive their degrees and end up as professional staff in government, industry, and academe. Often they show their gratitude for the time you have spent with them by directing work your way.

(2) When called for an interview for a newspaper or a magazine article, always spend time. My only insistence

is that the interviewer insert my name and the name of my newsletter or consulting firm in his article. A couple of years ago, in the span of three months, I was cited in *Scientific American, Omni,* and the *Washington Post.* Subscriptions to my newsletter, the *Washington Remote Sensing Letter (WRSL)* (I have three, more about the other two later), increased substantially following these citations. In 1990, *Space News,* an excellent weekly newspaper published in the Washington, D.C. area, featured a series of articles in satellite remote sensing, my own field of expertise. Instead of being put off by the fact that a competing news outlet was infringing on my turf, I consented to interviews that resulted in my name and the name of my newsletter being spread over several articles in the series. Subscriptions to *WRSL* are still rolling in as a result of this publicity, and I can't wait for them to run another series on remote sensing. In addition, I picked up some consulting work as well, whose origin I could track back to the *Space News* series. My general rule is, "An initial talk or contact is not only cheap, it is free." But once you want me to put pen to paper or slide to screen or words to audience, then pay you must.

9 KEEPING IT COOL AT THE WATER COOLER

Never trouble trouble till trouble troubles you

Working alone as a consultant means that sometimes you are hired to perform a task at your client's place of business. And so, for several days, weeks, or months you are appearing as a stranger in a strange land—a hired gun. Under those circumstances, there are three rules you *must* follow. Rule number one: Spend your time doing whatever it is you are being paid to do, and keep out of office politics. Rule number two: Keep out of office politics and spend your time doing whatever it is you are being paid to do, and Rule number three: Never forget rules number one and two. Am I beating it to death? Yes? Good! One of the (I thought) smartest (ex-) highly paid consultants I know got himself entangled in that great and sticky web of office politics. Finding himself "embroiled in a major imbroglio" between his client's systems engineering staff and marketing team, he unwisely chose a side (instead of stepping aside). When the smoke cleared, everyone hugged and kissed, blamed and fired the consultant, and continued on their merry way. Three simple, simple rules. Learn them well. I'll test you next week.

10 | WHEN TO WORK AND WHEN TO PLAY

Fun time, and a bit of a digression

In truth, when you are working alone you never really play. Of course, there will be some who will insist that when you work alone you are *always* at play. So who knows. Our youngest son, now in college, used to come home from high school in midafternoon, usually accompanied by his friends. In the blazing, sunny, June days, he would invariably find me on the deck, grabbing a tan. In response to his friends' natural supposition that I was either fired, laid off, retired, or just naturally lazy (after all, every one of their dads was then in an office downtown somewhere—managing, doctoring, lawyering, or elsewise making an "honest" living)—my son would say, "No, he's really working. He's a consultant." When pressed as to what I actually do, his response would be that I'm always thinking.

And this is true. Even when the lone consultant is as far removed as possible from the venue of his own and his clients' official workplace, there is a little corner in his head that is always Looking For Possibilities; Contemplating Opportunities, and Reliving Victories Won and Chances Lost. Because you have no one, in the business sense, that you can regularly depend on, you know in your heart of hearts that both successes and failures must be placed at your doorstep alone. A cartoon strip I keep taped to my office door says it well. It shows a lad behind his lemonade stand. Business is nonexistent, and he is saying

14

to himself, "When you run a one-man operation, the trouble is you can't put the blame on your employees when you have a bad day." So true, so true. Whatever income you bring in is derived entirely as a result of your own efforts. No efforts, no income. This means that if you're enjoying a play at the Kennedy Center or a concert at Wolf Trap or a flea market in Mount Airy, you're always plotting, even subconsciously, how you can convert something you are seeing into a business opportunity.

The flea market is a recent example. I am a "saver." I distinguish this from being a "collector," which is a much more honorable activity. Collectors are knowledgeable connoisseurs who specialize in specific items of interest. Savers, on the other hand, are undisciplined accumulators of "things." Any thing will do. For instance, when I was with the federal government (NASA), I saved used staples. Sounds strange, right? Well, you know some people save bits of string, or rubber bands, and construct monster balls of these items. Well, no one I knew saved used staples, and anyway, I felt that the inanity of some of the activities going on around me demanded an equally harmless activity of my own. Don't get me *too* wrong. I didn't spend the taxpayers' dollars by running around grabbing staples. On the other hand, whenever I pulled a staple from some sheets I had before me, I tossed it into the bottom right-hand drawer of my desk. It was no secret; everyone knew it. And every now and then a coworker would come up to my desk, wordlessly open the bottom right-hand drawer, and drop in a handful of used staples. By the time I quit the Fed, the drawer was full. I sold the staples to an associate for $20, and I have since heard that he sold them to another coworker for $50 when he transferred to the energy department. By then the staples filled three desk drawers. My guess is that there is now a legal-sized, four-drawer file cabinet filled with used staples hovering somewhere around NASA headquarters, under the auspices of a senior manager there. This might explain why NASA is having some problems with its flight programs. Everybody is out collecting used staples when they should be paying attention to technical details of their programs.

But I digress. As a "saver" I have managed to accumulate a mini-storage (10′ × 10′ × 10′) compound full of technical literature, reports, documents, magazines, journals, reprints, etc. These are being saved for posterity, or my demise, whichever comes first. Recently, at an enormous flea market in Mount Airy, Maryland, I saw a little old man (undoubtedly me in twenty or thirty years) sell a 1983 issue of *Scientific American* for 75 cents. Hmmm, I thought, I have 496 boxes of that stuff aging in a locked warehouse. Why has it been stored all this time? Because, I realized, I knew that I would eventually visit that flea market and see someone pay 75 cents for a decade-old technical magazine. Well, what I am going to do is this. At the very next opportunity, be it a shopping mall, a flea market, or a community garage sale, I am going to retrieve several boxes from storage, set up a table, place a small digital scale on the table, and charge—let's see—maybe $1.00 per pound for whatever anybody wants to buy. I've already designed a sign on my laser printer that says, "Techs Buck Company: Knowledge by the Pound." I'll let you know how it goes.

Now, I'm not saying that I *always* see things in terms of opportunities. But I must admit that it happens often enough to keep me smiling and all our bills paid. Also, it makes for a good deal of fun. I do believe that when you cannot distinguish between work and play, it really means that you are enjoying life, and that's probably more important than anything else.

11 | SAVING AND USING RECEIPTS

It's the little ones that count

One of the most onerous, but necessary, duties that you will have is to save all your receipts. The Internal Revenue Service, in fact, places very specific requirements on the minimum dollar amounts of receipts they require you to have. My own requirements are more stringent than those of the IRS. I said, "Save *all* receipts," and I mean exactly that. As a one-man operation, this may seem, at first, to be a too burdensome, nonsensical piece of mickey-mousery. But believe me, it's worth it.

Years ago, I was hired by the president of a small research company, who was having some organizational difficulties. He asked me to travel to his lab, interview his top management, and prepare a short report. The four-day job (two days for the interviews and two days for report-writing) was to be a one-shot affair, and I submitted my invoice along with the report. The invoice included my expenses, of course. And listed as an expense was an item, with a receipt, for thirty cents (yes, 30 cents). It was for a toll charge I incurred taking the rental car from the airport to his place of business. I must admit that I did flinch for a moment when I wrote in that thirty cents. In fact, when I copied the receipts for my files, I almost deleted that one. But no, I thought, it was a legitimate expense, no matter how small, and I included it.

Certainly, if it were noticed at all, it would result in one of three reactions: (1) Nothing would be said, it would be ignored; or (2) The customer would point out the item, view it with contempt, imagine that it reflects a definite lack of proportion on my part, and it would be the last I would hear from him; or (3) The customer would point out the item, view it with admiration, imagine that it reflects an admirable attention to detail on my part, and it would be the start of a long-term relationship.

Well, I've been consulting for that company for many years now, and although I can't state *positively* that it was that thirty-cent toll receipt that did it, I'm certain that it played a role far larger than its meager face value.

In general, I feel that you should claim all legitimate expenses, no matter how small. Further, if you claim an expense, no matter its size, that claim must be accompanied by a valid receipt. It keeps you straight, and just as important, it provides an appropriate paper trail for your client to his management, and everybody is kept happy.

12 | WHO COVERS EXPENSES? THE CUSTOMER DOES!

You pay for what I do, and what it costs me to do it

The initial (usually unspoken) reaction of many clients to a consultant's fee schedule is, "Wow! $2,000 per day. That's $730,000 per year—$732,000 on leap years." Well of course, a consultant doesn't work, or charge 365 (or 366) days a year. And we will provide a rather full discussion of fee schedules and the rationale for them on another page. I note it here because the client, if he concludes that your per diem rate is rather enormous, will no doubt rock back further when you immediately say, "plus expenses, of course." But you must say it. Expenses incurred by you in performance of your services to the client should in all cases be itemized and paid for by the client. Do not fall into the trap of agreeing to a somewhat higher per diem that includes your expenses. Without doubt and as certain as day follows night, you will find yourself being required to make that unbudgeted one-month trip to Kazakhstan on your own hook, and say goodbye to your bank account.

If your client insists on a flat fee, expenses-included contract, then you have no choice but to demand an artificially exorbitant price, and hope he signs on. If he refuses to meet your price, you have no choice but to decline the work. Low-balling an expenses-included contract is a true path to the poorhouse, and *you*, not the client will be to blame. On the other hand, if the client is willing to sign on to a higher-than-usual number, and cannot be dissuaded, then by all means go ahead and take his money. You have nothing to be ashamed of. An example follows:

Back several years, when the going rate for Washington, D.C. consultants was in the area of $500 per day, I was conducting a regular consultancy at that rate (plus expenses, of course) with a unit of a (very) large corporation headquartered in the southwest. One day I was contacted by a gentleman who represented another line of business within that corporation. He had sat in on a lecture I had given and wanted to secure my services for a short-term project.

Specifically, he wanted me to (1) provide an in-depth briefing to his staff on the capabilities, programs, and activities of three federal laboratories scattered around the United States; (2) set up meetings with the management of these laboratories for two of his staff, and accompany them to these meetings to participate in discussions with the lab directors; and (3) prepare a report summarizing the visits, including recommendations for a market penetration activity to be initiated by his organization.

This was to be a three-week effort, start to finish. I quoted him a fee of $7,500 (15 working days × $500) plus expenses. He insisted on my quoting a total package flat fee, including expenses. I told him that I would get back to him by close of business that day. This, by the way, is an important technique. Very few clients, or potential clients (actually, none that I have ever met), have demanded an immediate and instantaneous response to a proposal. In fact, by promising, and delivering a response within a given time period, you are indicating a sense of business maturity and acumen that a client will appreciate. Far better to go in with a thought-through response than to blurt out an expeditious and soon-to-be-retracted attestation.

At any rate, I added together current airline fares, hotel rates, telephone calls, car rental costs, etc. It came to $2,800. Together with my fee that came to $10,300. I looked at that total and added a contingency of 20 percent, or $2,060. That brought the total to $12,360. When I called the client back later that afternoon, I told him that I could do the job—fee plus expenses, the whole nine yards—for $22,000. He agreed on the spot. The work began two weeks later. Three weeks after that it was completed and the customer was happy. A month later (that particular company "aged" its invoices for four weeks; a practice I myself appreciate and follow) I received a check for $22,000, and *I* was happy.

13 | ATTENDING CONFERENCES

Meeting, greeting, and spreading the word

Whether you publish newsletters, are a consultant, or do both as do I, then attending conferences has to be one of your premiere activities. It is essential that you keep current in whatever field you would be called "expert." This means that you must follow the stream of conferences in your own, and closely allied fields. By "conferences," I include workshops, seminars, meetings, exhibits, etc. It is impossible, of course, to track and attend *all* events *everywhere*. My general rules are (1) Attend all meetings that take place in the Washington, D.C. area that may impact my business, and (2) Attend meetings elsewhere only if I am on a panel, presenting a paper, or having my expenses covered by a client or through some other means.

Most meetings (I exclude here those that are privately sponsored seminars for which a fee is charged) will allow a representative from the press to attend all sessions, with the presentation of appropriate press credentials. Without exception, I register and, to the extent possible, attend all technical conferences being held in Washington, D.C. One of my newsletters, the *Washington Federal Science Newsletter*, envelops a broad enough spectrum of subjects to include areas covered by most technical conferences held in the city. I attend these conferences when they do not conflict in time with any consulting activities I am currently undertaking.

22

Most meetings have a press room available, fully loaded with computers, snacks, and comfortable chairs and sofas. Registration (free) for the meeting is expedited in the press room, and all conference materials are made available to the press at no charge. These include a complete set of abstracts of talks being given, and press kits prepared by exhibitors. My first task is gathering together these materials and asking the person in charge of the press room to have them mailed to my office in the National Press Building. This means that I don't have to lug around bundles of technical papers all day. (Several days later the U.S. postal service delivers a large package of conference materials to me. I go through it all, discarding most, using some of it for my newsletter and some for my consulting activities. Some end up in a cardboard box that eventually gets packed away in a mini-storage warehouse, to be saved for some future use.) If a table is made available in the press room for distribution of literature (and it usually is), I place there several hundred brochures and subscription applications for my newsletter.

Unless I deem a particular session to be of direct and immediate import, I do not enter a room, sit down, and listen to a presentation. The reason is very simple. Working alone, you cannot be in more than one place at a time. If you spend the afternoon comfortably listening to a panel of eminent researchers discussing their latest papers from *Acta Retracta*, that means you have given up several hours of wandering the hallways and exhibits, where you may have met old friends, as well as strangers, who may have become new clients or subscribers. A *customer unmet* is an *account unbilled*. And as you are alone in the business world, surrounded by institutional enormity, it is incumbent upon you to touch as many people as you can. A conference, even sponsored by a local society chapter, much more, a national gathering, brings together the very people you have wanted to meet. Ordinarily, they are scattered about the country, unreachable. The conference has served to concentrate them, both in a spatial and temporal sense, and has provided you with the opportunity to meet as many as you can in the shortest possible time.

I have mentioned the exhibits and hallways. Your meanderings should also lead you to corporate reception rooms, hospitality suites, and hotel watering holes. The first two offer free food and drinks, items always of interest to someone working alone. Now some rather simple but important rules: (1) Never eat anything that can drip on you, and (2) Never eat anything that can stick between your teeth.

In view of these rules, I make it a habit of visiting a mirror every so often. Nobody will tell you that you've got a 2-mm piece of spinach pasted on your front tooth, and the smiles you get will give no hint that there is a dime-sized marinara splat on your shirt collar. One fellow I don't know trailed a foot-and-a-half long sheet of toilet paper from the back of his pants for the better part of a morning, till someone finally pointed it out to him. Let me tell you, that doesn't make what we call a positive impression.

14 | DRESSING FOR SUCCESS

To wear or not to wear . . .

In the world bounded by the Washington Beltway, where perception is often reality, you would undoubtedly expect me to come out strongly for a dress code that reeks of $70 silk ties, $200 Gucci shoes, and $900 suits (continental cut, of course). We all know that "clothes make the man," and you have but one opportunity to make a first impression. Indeed so. The argument is a simple one. Your potential client enhances his own self-esteem by associating himself with a well-dressed, well-appointed consultant. Conversely, if you appear before him in tattered slacks and a T-shirt, you substantially reduce the client's confidence in you before you say word-one, no matter the height and breadth of your intellectual reputation.

That said, be aware that I dress very much the same as I write (and very much the same as I do everything else, informally). The problem, as I saw it, was to establish a dress style broad enough to satisfy my own comfort zone, while at the same time provide the required high confidence signal to the client. I thought about that one long and hard. My own 'druthers lean to a casual life-style, and I ultimately felt that any unnatural constraint imposed upon me, however superficially beneficial, could in the long run only distract from my ability to amass, cultivate, and keep clients, customers, and subscribers.

As a federal government executive, I wore, daily, a business suit, a white shirt, and a rather conservative tie. For nine years I felt a distinct aversion to that style of dress. In fact, I must admit that in the waning days of my employ, I began slipping into my natural ways; First, I would eschew the business suit and wear a sport coat instead and then drifted into tieless sport shirts. Finally, in a fit of bravado, in my last weeks before I quit the Fed, I appeared in blue jeans and sweatshirt, my uniform of choice.

But one cannot imagine that I would appear before a client as a consultant or as a newsletter editor at a congressional hearing or as a reporter at a Washington press conference dressed in jeans and sweatshirt. Certainly not. (Well, not usually, anyway. There was at least one outstanding exception that I will relate elsewhere.)

Without going into specific details as to how I got to where I am (clothes-wise), my business wardrobe consists of three sports coats, five pairs of slacks, two pairs of shoes (one black, one brown), four pairs of sneakers, four sport shirts, fifteen ties, eight dress shirts, and one suit. I also own several dozen tie pins and lapel pins. I won't go through the rationale for accumulating this particular wardrobe, other than to note that by working alone you may have to (1) cover a significant number of geographically diverse locations in a single day or (2) remain at a single client's location for an extended period of time or (3) remain alone in your own office.

In any of these cases, the single overriding factor is your own comfort. I place this even above your client's perception. Indeed, once you have established yourself as to capability and reliability in that client's eye, then his positive perception of you will be reinforced by your cultivating a sense of relaxed informality. At least I feel that to be true in my own instance.

Serenity, contentment, ease of mind, and reduction of stress are the four corners of self-appreciation. And self-appreciation (not to be confused with self-centered arrogance) leads directly to self-confidence, which is the *sine qua non* for anyone working alone. I decided, finally, that a potential client would easily detect in me a quality of self-assurance that would quickly transcend any initially perceived discomfort due to the fact that I was not a power-suit-guy. So far it has worked out fine.

15 GOING WITH THE FLOW

You can't predict how a situation will end, no matter how strangely it begins

I follow rather carefully the ins and outs of the Washington technical scene, particularly as it concerns space-related activities. When I left NASA in October 1980, I immediately established a consulting firm, Associated Technical Consultants (ATC). In July 1981, I published Volume 1, Number 1 of the *Washington Remote Sensing Letter (WRSL)*. More about those two specific ventures in following pages.

By 1983 there was a major initiative under way by the Reagan administration to privatize, or commercialize, the nonmilitary remote sensing satellites then orbiting the earth. (Remote sensing refers to the acquisition and interpretation of space-derived photographs of the earth.) These satellites provide imagery of the earth that is used to map, monitor, and assess global resources, weather, and the environment. I have been involved with these satellites, the images they provide, and the policies surrounding their operation and management for many years. The satellites had been managed by an operational agency of the U.S. Department of Commerce (DOC) called the National Oceanic and Atmospheric Administration (NOAA). The satellites were about to be placed on the auction block, and a hasty press conference was called when the administration decided to make a formal announcement to that effect. This is big news to someone who publishes a remote sensing newsletter.

I was out in my back yard, in suburban Maryland, making little logs out of big logs, when the phone in my

28

back pocket rang. Hmmm, a slight digression here. True, most people don't do yard work with a cellular telephone tucked into their back pockets. But then again, most people don't work alone; they have a visible and comprehensive support organization and structure always close at hand. I do, of course, have telephone answering machines, but much better to take calls live then to return calls, no matter how rapid your response to a message left on a machine.

The phone call was from the public affairs officer at DOC, and he informed me that a press conference was being held in thirty minutes to announce the decision to sell the U.S. civilian remote sensing satellite system to the highest bidder. Again, this was big news, and promised significant impact on both my newsletter and my consulting business, and I wasn't about to miss the show. It was early afternoon, but even going against the minimum traffic on I-270, it was still a half-hour trip downtown to the commerce department. With no time to change, I flew down the highway and arrived at the press conference just as the briefing officer began to read his statement. That person, the associate administrator of NOAA responsible for the U.S. weather and land satellites, glanced up as I came in. In a room filled with television cameras, reporters, and broadcast and print journalists, all well-suited (literally), I stood out in my blue jeans and sweatshirt, press credentials dangling from a chain around my neck. There was some raising of eyebrows amongst my peers, which I ignored. The NOAA official, a gentleman I knew well from my NASA days, said, "Good afternoon, Murray, I'm glad you could join us. We can begin now." I said, "Thank you for waiting, John, go right ahead." He smiled, I smiled, and as I looked around the room, the disdain I had earlier detected was quickly replaced by glances of what I can only describe as pure envy. It's the same sort of journalistic jealousy that permeates the White House briefing room when the President recognizes a reporter by his name, but here, on a smaller scale. The result, though, is the same. The listening audience automatically generates a conclusion that the individual is an insider, "in the know," and privy to information not generally available to others. All of this is positive input into the life of the consultant or newsletter publisher.

Following the reading of the announcement, I let some of my fellow journalists ask the usual bland questions that are invariably asked of government officials at press conferences. I was then recognized and asked my NOAA friend what could be called a set of penetratingly difficult questions. He began his response by saying, "The problem, Dr. Felsher, is that you know too much . . ." That did it. Afterwards, I was approached by a reporter from National Public Radio, who was covering the news conference. We scheduled an interview on the subject of the news conference for the following day, and it was aired on NPR's "All Things Considered" that evening. *WRSL* subscriptions surged for the following two weeks, all of which I credit to that interview. When the official commerce department transcript of the news conference was distributed, it of course contained the NOAA official's reference to the fact that I knew too much. I still use that quote in my direct marketing mailouts, and I will use it forever.

16 | ATC

Affirm a firm firmly

On October 4, 1980, Associated Technical Consultants was born. It had a long gestation period, swimming around the back of my head for years while I worked as a technocrat in the Washington, D.C. headquarters offices of the U.S. Environmental Protection Agency (EPA) and then the National Aeronautics and Space Administration (NASA). In both agencies I often came across individuals who were hired by large consulting firms on government contracts. These individuals, themselves consultants, were hired to help us. More often than not, they knew far less about the subject for which they were hired than did we federal executives ourselves. In fact, I would be regularly "interviewed" by these consultants. These interviews would invariably be briefing sessions by *me* for *them*. As it turned out, I was drawing a salary from the U.S. taxpayer to educate an ignorant consultant, so that he could prepare a report and sell it back to me, often containing the very words of wisdom I myself imparted to him. Hmmm . . . Such a deal!

What if, I thought, the consultant was *really* good. I mean, what if he really knew his stuff and didn't have to depend on reticent bureaucrats to educate him. (And here I must admit that, out of resentment, I always held back information from a consultant, especially if I felt that I was providing his grade school education, and I usually was.) I began seriously to consider the possibility

31

of abandoning the federal arena and entering the consulting world. I knew that I knew my subject. I knew that I had, over the years, created a broad network of peers that might readily be transformed into a viable client base. A major point of consideration was evaluating my true worth to an interested client. Could I approach someone in the public or private sector, offer to "rent out" my brain for a period of time, and find any takers? Would anyone be interested in what I knew *and be willing to pay for that knowledge?* Would they pay enough to justify my removing myself from what is, in essence, a secure, lifelong job with a comfortable pension? My answers to all these and more questions would have to be a confident "yes" before I could jeopardize my family's and my own future.

Well, the long gestation period served to convince me that a move out of the federal government and into the private sector was indeed the right move to make. I was also convinced that I did not want to associate myself with any existing corporate enterprise, no matter its size or the range of its salary structure. As with many decisions I was to make, and still do make, the rationale behind this decision was not entirely logical. I have always proceeded according to "gut feel," a wholly unquantifiable and irrational process that one must simply accept and not attempt to explain. It may be perceived by others as self-confidence, though it really is quite more than that. In the face of sometimes significant setbacks, both tactical and strategic, it never really waivers. There is always an expectation of success, and invariably success follows.

Without benefit of a model or knowledge of the pitfalls, I created ATC. It was really a very simple thing to do. I rented a post-office box close to my home. I selected the name, Associated Technical Consultants, because it imparted a sense of stability, if not size, and implied that there indeed was an association of some kind backing me up. Of course there was none (there still is none). Further, the letters A, T, C seemed to roll easily off the tongue when spoken. I registered the "ATC Group" as a DBA

(doing business as) entity and received a federal identi-
fication number, for tax purposes, from the IRS. I then
had a set of business cards printed, and the box number
became the address on my business card. I elected myself
"president" of ATC, and had that title placed beneath my
name on the business card, again providing comfort for
those who would do business only with the top man. I then
had letterhead and envelopes printed. The letterhead has
on the bottom the printed message: "Associated Technical
Consultants is Affiliated with the ATC Group," which it is.
Again, this implied, to those who required it, a substantial
organizational backup. I should also note that any further
enterprises I was to create would also have an A, T, C
name, and that letterhead would also carry the same bottom
message. An example is Advanced Teaching Concepts—
but more about that later.

(At this point I must state that all the above was created
to impart an initial perception of ATC's reality, stability,
and reliability in the eyes of a potential client. But none
of that is of any avail if you are incapable of producing
the work expected, and having it paid for by the client.
You are being paid to perform a specific function. As a
consultant you sign a contract that obliges you to an exact
deliverable on an exact date. No business card or stationery,
however clever, credible, or *in*credible, will compensate for
a job poorly executed or tardily delivered. *Your name and
your reputation are only as good as the last piece of work
you have submitted.* And make no mistake, your reputation
will very quickly be enhanced or destroyed, depending
only on the quality and timeliness of the work you perform. And as a consultant working alone, you can make
a serious error [be it of fact or of judgment] only once.
The word will spread like wildfire throughout the community, and you will find yourself out in the street with
no clients and no income. And this goes quite beyond the
consultant's technical presentation. In areas such as ethical
behavior, confidentiality, and trust, a consultant must be
totally and squeakingly clean, without a hint of impro-
priety.)

Finally, and with some effort, I created a resume that I was satisfied with. I mailed out (first-class) a resume, a notice of my having left NASA, a cover letter announcing the establishment of ATC, and a business card to every one of the 1,100 names on my Rolodex. As this was done in late 1980, the actual mechanics would be considerably different had I been starting out in the 1990s. In particular, the desktop computer was not yet a reality (can that be true?). Today the word processing software products available for your Mac or PC, with its mailmerge capability and multitude of type fonts, sizes, and styles easily facilitate the creation of letters, stationery, and resumes. The laser printer allows you to produce final camera-ready copy that is easily edited. And in many cases you can omit the professional printer entirely by producing material on your own copying machine. Suffice it to say that today's technology provides you with a massive capability that you must take advantage of in order to minimize your "housekeeping" duties and maximize your money-making potential.

The major reason for broadcasting my resume around the landscape was to inform everyone I knew (and many I didn't know) that I was available. Of only secondary importance at this stage was the expectation that somebody would immediately want to hire me for a consulting job. For many readers this massive mail-out might seem like a somewhat crass and self-promoting activity. And if you were to accuse me of such activities, I would not only admit it, I would admire you for recognizing it, and admonish you for not appreciating it. Remember please, again and again and again: *Working alone, you and you alone are responsible for you and you alone.* You needn't apologize for making as many people as possible aware of your availability and capabilities. No apologies will be necessary if you succeed, and no apologies will be sufficient if you fail. Admittedly, it does take a different kind of person to undertake this sort of a venture.

I still send out, unsolicited, ATC flyers and my own resume. They pop out of my laser printer regularly and span the world. The vast majority end up as a crumpled wad in a circular file, unread. Some are first read, then wadded up. A few lead to responses, discussions, and would you believe it, actual consulting opportunities. And listen, if you need some help in establishing your *own* consulting business, call me up. My rates are reasonable, we're a stable and reliable organization. Have you ever heard of the ATC Group? Well, Associated Technical Consultants is affiliated with the ATC Group. Surely you've heard of them.

17 | HERE THERE BE DRAGONS

A word to my federal friends

Map makers of old, when faced with massive empty spaces of unknown geography, drew fanciful beasts and doodles. Occasionally, if a really large empty space presented itself, the cartographer would draw in, with his best calligraphic swirls, the phrase, "Here There Be Dragons."

I reserve these next few words for my fellow civil servants who would cast off their yoke of federal employ and seek the freedom, fulfillment, and fortune that accompanies the life of the lone consultant. Beware, beware, for in that great vacuity, there indeed may, for many of you, "be dragons." And these dragons gobble up consultants at an appalling rate. Without intending to fill your hearts with fear, but merely inserting a reality check at this point, there are several things you must know. First, the gray, well-marked, well-traveled four-lane highway that marks federal employ is totally unlike the beautiful, directionless, empty, country lane that is the world of the lone consultant.

And here I must insert some words about the typical federal bureaucrat, particularly the kind that inhabits an agency headquarters office in Washington, D.C. There really are two distinct and separate beasts, civil servants and political appointees. For purposes of the ensuing discussion, I am ignoring the latter—they will have their turn elsewhere in these pages. The vast majority of civil servants, and nearly all mid- to high-level managers suffer from a major debilitating illness called "defensive-itis." No matter how intelligently aggressive, idealistic, and bushy-tailed he might have been upon entering federal service, the civil servant bureaucrat, after passage of years and growth of perquisites, spends more and more of his time protecting his turf, and less and less of his time producing anything. Except paper, that is. As a bureaucrat climbs the federal food chain, the amount of paper attributable to him (most actually written by his subordinates, to which he claims authorship) manifoldly increases. The ultimate examples are the whole libraries that must be created to store, exhibit, and make available for researchers a President's papers when he leaves office.

The federal manager's activity described above is manifested by a characteristic withdrawal into his own shell as he spends more and more of his creative time building walls and moats and turrets around his bureaucratic empire. This serves to separate him more and more from events and people that surround him. At age fifty to sixty or so, after twenty or thirty years of frustrating federal service, he is a veteran of hundreds of bureaucratic battles, having won many medals with oak-leaf clusters for infighting and backbiting. His reward, the Holy Grail, which he has never lost sight of, is now within his reach. It's called a federal pension. When he is finally given the obligatory retirement luncheon at a local restaurant or an officer's club, he knows very few people outside his own speciality, little of the federal world outside his own office, and virtually nothing of the way the private sector operates. Such a person is doomed to failure should he attempt to start a one-man operation. And several people I know have suffered for having attempted to build a new career that requires an extrovert's confidence, after having spent a lifetime "hunkering down."

The only way to even hope for success working alone, coming from this debilitating environment, is to plot an early escape from the federal stranglehold. My own escape came after nine years, a period of time long enough to teach me a bit about the federal world, but short enough to not be seduced by its promise of pensioned prosperity. I still walked down the middle of a hallway, and watched older men and women sulk along the walls, hoping no one would see them or talk to them. In that arena, the ends of the bell curve, the really good and the awfully bad, soon leave federal employ, the former by choice and the latter by adverse action. That leaves a median population of executives that hovers about the "average," in all aspects of the word. It may be too harsh to cite this as a prime reason for *expecting* mediocrity as the concluding effort for any civil service operation, but it is close to the truth. One moves ahead in any bureaucratic venue by outlasting one's comrades, not making waves, and doing precisely and unimaginatively what one is told to do. The end result is that a civil servant sees no good coming from extended interaction with others—all such interactions are threatening and are viewed as lose-lose situations.

If you are to succeed alone, then your tenets must be diametrically opposed to what I have just described. You must be willing to meet with people, talk to people, learn from people, inform people, get to know people, and let them get to know you. This is a paradigm insurmountably difficult to overcome by too many people having spent too many years in federal employ. The world of the lone consultant is a too-exciting, dicey world for most, with too few signposts and too many beasts about. But for the few St. Georges out there, turn this way and I'll let you in on a secret—*dragons are a figment of the imagination.*

18 | BOLTS FROM THE BLUE— UPS AND DOWNS

Keep dropping seeds—most fall on concrete, but a few find warm, dark soil, and that's all you'll need

DOWNer: Two weeks after I mailed out my consulting announcements, relating to the world that I was available, I received a call from an official of the Office of Technology Assessment (OTA). OTA is the research arm formed by the U.S. Congress to provide background research on topics of interest to the members. For countless years before the creation of OTA, congressmen had been solely dependent upon professional lobbyists to provide them with data associated with legislation directly related to the interests of those very same lobbyists.

When I was contacted by OTA, Congress was gathering data related to the impending commercialization of the U.S. civilian satellite system, a topic I was more than familiar with. The director of the OTA office that dealt with space activities was a gentleman I knew. When his call came I assumed it was to wish me luck in my new venture. You can imagine my delight when he asked me to visit him in his Pennsylvania Avenue office to discuss a consulting contract. Our visit was most fruitful and positive. I provided an outline of the work I thought should be undertaken. We agreed on a statement of work, fee, and deliverable schedule. Less than a month out of the chute, and I was about to get a major piece of work. Hey, this was easier than I could ever have hoped. I floated past the Capitol, down to Union Station to catch the metro back to Shady Grove station, where I had left my car. (I still hadn't started my first newsletter, and so did not have a downtown office and was working out of my home.) To make a short story grim, I received a call the next day from the same gentleman, informing me that there had been a reprogramming effort underway, and the study I was to undertake for him was being postponed for three months. But not to worry, because I was still his man.

Two months later he had transferred to a new job at the National Academy of Sciences, doing work totally unrelated to any of my own expertise. When, indeed, a month after that, OTA undertook the study I had outlined, his replacement at OTA brought in another consultant to undertake it.

UPper: You may never know by what route a consulting job may wend its way to you. You may never be able to re-create a paper trail between an initial contact with person A, who then meets person B and mentions your name to him, and thence to C—a process replicated an unknown number of times that eventually leads to a call from person Z offering you a consulting job. Some two years ago I was called in by an aerospace company to conduct a half-day seminar. They had heard of me through a retired federal official. Back in 1983, when he was a high-ranking NASA administrator, I had introduced him to the head of another federal agency and had set up a meeting between the two. I did this *gratis*, but expected that any joint program that might be established between the two agencies would have a piece set aside for me as a consultant. As it turned out, no such joint program was agreed upon. But I was not forgotten. The NASA official, some six years later, remembered me to the aerospace company and recommended me for what we both thought would be a half-day's work. I am still on contract with that company, and to this day have netted more than $30,000 in consulting fees.

DOWNer: The woman sitting next to me on the flight to Washington National Airport was in her thirties-to-fifties (I can never tell), well-dressed, and talkative. She was returning from Newark, New Jersey, having attended a meeting of program grantees at a nearby state university. She was a mid-level manager at the (old) Department of Health, Education, and Welfare (HEW, now restructured as Health and Human Services, HHS), responsible for a $25-million activity. She was particularly upset at the way her meeting had gone, and the talk soon turned to ways that she might have structured the meeting to get more positive results. Actually, the talk really didn't *turn* that way, I had *steered* it that way. I had some experience organizing meetings of the very same kind as she was attempting to run. From the beginning, I viewed her as somewhat naive, and after confidently establishing my own credentials I presented her with my card, made several general observations, and asked for an appointment to discuss with her a consulting contract. If all of this sounded rushed, please believe that it was; the flight from Newark Airport to Washington National Airport is fleeting. She was apparently eager to oblige, and asked me to stop by her office the very next day.

I worked through the night, and as it was a prelude to the consummation of a consulting agreement, I did not feel obliged to charge her a fee for the day's work. (Did I mention that I was somewhat naive myself in those days?) Our meeting lasted much of the day, during which time I laid out a whole plan for her, including a detailed, step-by-step analysis of the pitfalls she would encounter and my suggested remedies. She said she was pleased and would get back to me quickly with a consulting agreement. To again make a short story grim, she never did get back to me. After several calls to her were not returned, her secretary finally did call to let me know that she was not interested in speaking with me. Pride alone requires me to assume that I had my brain cleanly and neatly picked by an expert, at no charge to our government. The only good thing that came out of that encounter was a promise I made to myself never to let anything like that happen to me again—and it never has.

19 | DOING WHAT COMES NATURALLY

Brie is not for me

In keeping with my preference for a casual life-style, described elsewhere, I am, frankly, most at home among comfortable, relaxed folk. You will not be surprised to learn that I don't own a tuxedo. You may be surprised to learn that I do drive a Corvette. My only vice. My wife calls it my mid-life-crisis car, although she would be the first to agree that I'm far too young at heart to have reached mid-life. As to a *crisis*, I haven't met one that is permanent enough to involve more than a small amount of brain cells for the shortest possible time.

As you work alone, there is a singular attribute that must permeate your being if you are to succeed at what you are trying to do. Namely, you must accede to alterations in your life-style, and accept the fact that, within your given framework of reference, you will indeed change. Further, you must understand that any profound change will be incorporated into your very existence, and you will, in the end, be better for it.

One of my first major consulting contracts began with an initial presentation to a large industrial corporation. The contract required me to be at the client's out-of-town location two to three nights per week for several months. The company made all my living arrangements (I now make them all myself). I knew something was a bit different when I was picked up at the airport by the hotel limo. The limo was a top-of-the-line Jaguar, driven by a uniformed chauffeur who was fluent in several languages, one of which might have been English. The hotel was a converted luxury apartment house, where my client had reserved for me a large, antique-furnished suite. The hotel boasted a four-diamond restaurant, the only one in the city, adept at haute cuisine, *tres* haute cuisine. Even the water was high in calories.

I was very uncomfortable with the living arrangements from the first, but decided not to mention this discomfort to my corporate contact. Undoubtedly, they were going all out to impress me with their *largesse*, and I didn't want to seem ungrateful or unappreciative. I felt that by hurting their feelings I could only damage my own consulting future with that company. How were they to know that I hate French food, rich sauces, belly-numbing desserts, and antique furniture. Well, one month and fourteen pounds later, as I felt my body, mind, and work suffering from terminal sluggishness, I finally 'fessed up and begged them to send me to the nearest Marriott. They agreed immediately, as it meant saving themselves more than one hundred dollars a day room and board. They felt much better. I did too, in more ways than one.

The "one-month gorging" (that's how I remember it) changed my life dramatically. That event took place nine years ago. In the ensuing years, I have, in sequence: (1) stopped imbibing alcohol, (2) stopped eating red meat, (3) stopped eating fowl, and (4) three years ago stopped eating seafood. I guess that makes me a vegetarian. Each morning my wife and I get up at 5:30 A.M. and briskly walk four-plus miles, I with a five-pound weight in each hand. As I write this in a Marriott Hotel in upper New York State, there is a canvas bag at my side containing the weights, and tomorrow morning I will take off for my "hour-power" walk before using the hotel gym. The executive floor at the hotel offers a free breakfast, but I'll skip it because I know that the board meeting I am attending at 8:00 A.M. will include a small buffet. All this is not to say that if you take care of yourself you will be automatically immune to the sea of germs, bacteria, and viruses in which we live. No indeed. But so far I'm feeling good. And when you work alone, you've *got* to feel good, because if you don't feel good, you can't work, and if you don't work, you don't get paid. Consultants don't get sick leave.

20 DATA, DATA, WHO HAS THE DATA?

Step one on the path to wisdom is data acquisition

The conversion of a bitstream of data into a slug of information, thence into a modicum of knowledge defines a continuum that, culminating in wisdom, encompasses the intellectual universe of the consultant. The chasm that exists, however, between acquiring data and imparting wisdom is wide, dark, and fraught with perils and pitfalls. Many very smart people have failed to recognize the difference between data and wisdom, and in attempting to bridge the chasm between the two, they have misstepped and found themselves plummeting into the depths of ignorance. (Wow! how is that for a vivid mind-picture?)

Run-on sentences aside, the consultant cannot hope to impart wisdom to his client if he is unable to acquire adequately the accurate and precise data he needs to do the job. The task is doubly difficult for a consultant working alone, since he cannot segment the work units by assigning data acquisition to someone, information transformation to another, and knowledge integration to still another member of his team. The lone consultant must exercise authority over every aspect of the continuum, an always difficult, and sometimes impossible task. It is imperative that he recognize the fact that the very first step, that of data acquisition, is often the most difficult step of all. The reason is that our present world of data storage and retrieval technologies, data handling and management strategies, and data delivery options, coupled with advanced telecommunications capabilities, often result in a glut, rather than a lack of data. Selective acquisition becomes a necessity for any worker seeking raw material for his information grist. For the lone consultant, selective acquisition becomes a first requirement.

It is easy to don the passive mode of a disinterested observer, soaking up everything offered to you by your senses. I call this the "blotter mode." And at times when you have, for whatever reason, turned your mental switch to "receive only," you may indeed, and very accidentally, acquire significant data. In truth, it is impossible to always be in a pro-active stance. Body and mind simply won't hear of it, and both insist on periods of waking relaxation. It is what I believe to be a natural attempt by our organic engine to extend its owner's warrantee and prevent premature burnout. When, from time to time, I feel myself downshifting mentally, I simply let it happen, and just lean back in the "blotter mode." Recently, I had just completed a study paper for a client, and was relaxing at the United Airlines Club in Dulles International Airport, going over a final draft of the report. I was flying to another client, and had arrived at the airport early (as I always do, and that will be the subject of another discussion), and leaned back, orange juice in hand. Just then the gentleman seated on the sofa behind me rose and called out to a Navy captain, just appearing in view, to join him. I switched to "receive only," expecting nothing but small talk. Instead, they undertook a very comprehensive, specific, and analytical discussion that ranged from J-3 and J-5 activities at the Joint Strategic Command in Offutt Air Force Base, to the six-way bypass performed on the Emir of Bahrein, then ensconced in Blair House. They didn't speak loudly, but neither did they whisper. They perhaps were not intimidated by my proximity to them; I was wearing my usual jeans and sweatshirt. Evidently I posed no threat, for they kept on for fifteen minutes or so till Navy left for his flight. I don't expect that any "classified" material was being discussed openly; at least I hope not. But the quantity, if not quality, of tidbits you can pick up this way never ceases to amaze me. And if you are the kind that amasses these tidbits for future analysis and interpretation, life can be very interesting indeed.

And here I must insert a word or two about the ethics involved in overhearing a conversation, as I did in the above instance. I clearly differentiate "overhearing" from "eavesdropping." The former is an accidental, unintentional, and passive activity I relish. The latter is a conceived, planned, and an active undertaking I abhor. I look forward to overhearing tidbits. But I consider it unacceptable (not to mention immoral, unethical, and possibly illegal) for a consultant to acquire a data set in any manner that can be construed as eavesdropping.

In that connection, it seems reasonable to expect that a person willing to work alone will have a personality trait that allows him to respond to accidental events in a manner designed to enhance his future opportunities. In the example just given, I might very well have stood up and walked away when it became apparent that I would be overhearing another's private conversation—that is true. But the onus was not on me; I neither planned nor initiated the activity. Neither did I move it along in any way. I cite the following event as a similar example, but with a bit of a twist and a heck of a difference: We once had a telephone number which was one digit away from the local supermarket, and for the six months we lived at that address we received at least a half-dozen calls a week by mis-dialers who were interested in something or other at the supermarket. For the first month I politely disclosed to the caller that he had mis-dialed. For the following five months the conversations went something like this:

CALLER: "Hello. What are your bakery hours?"

ME: "Sorry, we're closed till next Monday, the baker ran away with the dough." Hang up, or,

CALLER: "Hello. What is your special on donuts?"

ME: "Three dozen for a dollar, but you have to buy ten gross." Hang up, or,

CALLER: "Hello. Where exactly are you located?"

ME: "We're right on the corner of 'Walk' and 'Don't Walk.'" Hang up.

You get the idea. The difference is that although the action was initiated by another person, I moved the situation along by taking action of my own. I should also add that in one or two serious instances, as when the caller was seeking information on medication and prescriptions, I did inform them that they had the wrong number. Taking advantage of a situation by providing myself with some harmless amusement, as in the case above, stems from a very similar personality trait that allows me to overhear a conversation and take advantage of data unknowingly and provided through no action of my own. So, again, I have no qualms about "accidentally" acquiring data, and urge you to similarly accept such data when the circumstance arises.

The accidental acquisition of data, however, is the exception to the rule. Usually you will be seeking data explicitly related to a task you have been hired to undertake. I have always maintained an old-fashioned vertical file that covers everything I have ever worked on. Whenever I come across an article, news release, report, or any document of interest to me, I incorporate it into the file. When I started doing this, as a graduate student, more than thirty years ago, I used to fill out a small ($3'' \times 5''$) card with the basic bibliographic data and short two or three sentences describing the item. When the desk-top computer arrived I began to convert all my paper files into computer files. I began this more than eight years ago, and have not only failed to keep up, I have fallen far behind. In a perfect world, if a client would be interested, say, in tracking the history of radar satellites, I could punch in a word or two on my Macintosh, and for the next half-hour the machine would spew out reams of data. In our imperfect world, however, mirrored by my own imperfections, of course, I scurry from file cabinet to computer, from library reference to telephone inquiry, and from memory to memorabilia. After much anguish and luck, along with determined promises to get everything quickly computerized (though I know I never will), I end up with a stack of data that I have compiled related to the task at hand.

The size of the stack, in inches, feet, or meters, is roughly proportional to the size of the fee I am charging the client. I have found that most of the time taken to impart wisdom to a client is with the initial acquisition of the data. The transformation of data into information and the integration of the information into a knowledge base are certainly more gratifying tasks in terms of intellectual satisfaction. But if the appropriate data are not inserted at the front end of the system, then any amount and quality of analysis, however sublime, elegant, and massive, will result in an invalid conclusion. It's the computer programmer's old acronym—GIGO—garbage in, garbage out.

The task for the consultant working alone, then, is twofold, and can be compressed to the phrase, "validate selective data." A smaller amount of correct data, crisply analyzed, is worth far more to the client (and to yourself, in the long run) than an historically interminable report whose fuzzy conclusions are based on reams of questionable data. I remember very clearly sitting through a two-hour viewgraph briefing by a consultant with (hitherto) impeccable credentials, which grew wearier, and more and more unfocused as time passed. It became painfully obvious that his monumental conclusions were proportional to the weight (squared) of his data. As a consultant, you must know beyond doubt that you will never fool anyone by substituting rhetoric for fact.

Rule One will always be to spend the maximum time possible acquiring the initial data upon which your subsequent work will be based, and Rule Two is if these data are truly not available, then you must report this to your client. Consultants have a great deal of difficulty admitting that they are unable to secure the data needed to satisfy the client. Some will foolishly plunge ahead, constructing a mountain of conclusions from a sand grain of fact. Danger, danger. Far better to contact the client and inform him that the data needed for his particular requirement are simply not available. He must accept this knowledge (and will usually appreciate it), and the very fact that a data set are not available may itself be the conclusion that he is seeking. And if you have been clever in constructing your consulting agreement, the client will still be obliged to pay you for the time you have spent on his project, regardless of the outcome.

21 AIDING PERCEPTION

Sending a message, I

Sometimes a potential client sends me a signal that says, "I have wealth, I have power, I have substance. And what's more I deal only with people who have wealth, power, and substance, and that goes for consultants I hire as well." The signal can be a mere raised eyebrow at seeing my rather small, cluttered office in the National Press Building. Or it can be an openly rude question, innocently asked, like "What sort of car do you drive?" When I determine that such a signal has been transmitted, I am quick to receive and respond. The response, especially if I am already not interested in pursuing work with that client, takes the form of a quick goodbye. Or, if I'm in a wicked mood, I will ask him for a quick loan of a couple thousand. The result is the same; he's gone.

However, there are times when I do want the client to perceive me as a person of wealth, power, and substance (which I am not). This is especially true if I am interested in working for him as a consultant. In those instances I manage to display, as necessary, one or all of the three props I carry for just that purpose. Without dwelling on any, these are (1) a $500 leather attache case, (2) a $300 Mont Blanc fountain pen, and (3) a platinum American Express card. After our meeting I then offer to drop him off at his next appointment, and steer him into the passenger seat of my Corvette. That usually does the trick. Most of these wealth, power, and substance guys tool around town

in their Beamers, Mercedes, and similar cars. When they
leave the Corvette they're usually breathless and bubbling,
and their perception of me melds into their perception
of themselves. I don't mind, as long as I don't have to
wear a tux.

22 | TRAVELING LIGHT

Bulk does not a winner make

The Sierra Club admonishes us to " . . . take only pictures and leave only footprints." A consultant should present his client with a final report, collect his fee, and depart the premises cleanly, having spent his time unfettered by excess baggage, both literally and figuratively. In the context of this book, then, I would have you take only fees and leave only paper. Traveling light has become a cliché, but a valid one nonetheless. A general rule is *If it doesn't fit under the seat in front of you, then stow it in the overhead bin; if it doesn't fit in the overhead bin, then leave it at home.*

There will be exceptions, but I can remember only once having checked luggage on a business trip. And that was a one-week stay in Trieste, Italy. (Family vacations however, are another story. When our three children were young, it would take two skycaps to move the five of us from the taxi to the check-in counter.)

I have for years and years traveled light, and I urge you to travel even lighter, coming or going. The very first reason is that as a lone consultant you bring with you but two arms. And if each arm is pained with excess luggage, and your shoulders are strained from small bags strapped around your neck, you are imposing additional burdens on yourself that your body will remember and repay. To coin a phrase, "the lighter the baggage the freer the mind."

What you bring with you to a client is your own competence, capability, and creativity. These are your ultimate currencies of value. You may indeed have an extensive subject library somewhere at your disposal, backing you up, but the consultant who arrives at his client's office ready to begin work carrying five cartons of books is immediately suspect. The client will wonder why he is paying a large fee to a person who is merely citing other peoples' research. Never mind that the consultant may be integrating several avenues of information, and thus creating a special new knowledge base for the client. The client will not necessarily understand this, and may believe that one of his own employees (who is earning a much lower daily salary than the consultant) can accumulate the same literature and do the job without the consultant's help.

Further, it is important to understand that the client, at all times, must have total confidence in what you tell him. It's not like baseball, where a .333 lifetime batting average will likely get you into the Hall of Fame. For a consultant, that would mean that you were *wrong* two times out of three. And would you put your life in the hands of a surgeon who batted .500? Well, technical consultants fall somewhere between high-powered lawyers and thoracic surgeons, in terms of expected success. Once the client has even the smallest seed of doubt planted in his mind as to your abilities, you are history.

Bring your brain. The client will provide you with whatever materials you might need, and free of charge, I might add. The wisdom you offer to the client will have emerged from your own creative endeavors as integrated knowledge. If you have what it takes, then success will follow. And if you can't cut the mustard, then any and all appurtenances will serve you naught. I know a consultant who traveled to his client's Ohio office with a trunk full of writing pads, stapler, ruler, floppy disks, pens, pencils, scotch tape, telephone message pads, thesaurus, dictionary, manila file folders, telephone answering machine, a small technical library, and everything but his tax accountant. He had hoped to make an impression as a completely self-sufficient individual. Instead, he impressed the client as someone who could easily be diverted from points of central importance to Trivia Alley. He lasted a day. And the only reason I am able to cite the details is that the very same client told me the story when he hired me as replacement. All I brought with me was my attaché case.

23 LOBBYING, CONSULTANT STYLE

Diversions and excursions

Especially since you are working alone, you will need a short mental break, every now and then. The difficulty is that you can't mosey over to the water cooler, lean up against the wall, and talk small talk with whoever happens to occupy the neighboring space. In *your* office *nobody* occupies the neighboring space. This means you must create several different diversions and excursions to provide a change in your workday rhythm. I myself have several such break-a-days, and one of them is lobbying. I don't mean to imply that I am a registered lobbyist. Certainly, I do drift up Capitol Hill, but I do not spend more than five percent of my time buttonholing congressmen and senators, trying to influence legislation (I believe that's the official definition of a lobbyist.)

Actually, I'm talking about *office building* lobbies. Really. One of my newsletters, *Defense Contract Awards (DCA),* is geared to the multitude of Beltway Bandits, as we call them, that hover throughout the Washington, D.C. area contracting paper studies for federal government agencies. I guess my own consulting firm, ATC, is one of these, and so I use the BB words with no insult intended (though outside the beltway, *i.e.*, the rest of the world, Beltway Bandit *is* used with some aspersion). *DCA* is a biweekly listing of contracts awarded by the U.S. Department of Defense (DOD), and as with my other newsletters, I am always looking for new subscribers.

My newsletter office is in the National Press Building, in the heart of downtown DC. I've a two-minute walk to the Mall, a three-minute walk to the White House, a ten-minute walk to the Capitol, and I'm surrounded by office buildings housing thousands of potential newsletter subscribers. Only I don't know who they are. As a routine diversion I will step out of my office building, walk this way or that for a few, or several, or many minutes, depending on my 'druthers, and randomly enter an office building. Sometimes I will drive around a bit before I select a building. (In that event, the diversion becomes an excursion.)

At this point I should tell you that Washington, D.C. office buildings are a breed apart. I mean, if you go into a New York, or Chicago, or Los Angeles office building, it may be 40 or 50 or 60 stories high, with hundreds, if not thousands, of occupants. Well, as you might expect, things are different in Washington, D.C. There is a federally enacted legal upper limit to the height a building in Washington, D.C. can reach. Practically, this law restricts heights of Washington, D.C. buildings to roughly 150 feet, which is some 12 to 14 stories. Many feel, as do I, that this gives a small-town, warm appeal to downtown Washington, and sets off the business centers of the District of Columbia from the green, rectangular Mall; from the stark, gray federal buildings; and from the sparkling white monuments. It is a downtown of clean, wide, tree-lined streets, bordered by a peneplained horizon, with all buildings reaching the same height.

However, thus prevented from expressing their creativity vertically, architects here have turned to impressively varied means of differentiating their own structures from the guy's next door. Many find the result boorish, vulgar, or bourgeois. Me, I like it; I delight in exploring the many new buildings popping up all over the downtown area, around the Beltway, and alongside the interstates.

Besides the aesthetic pleasure I receive when visiting a newly occupied office building, I also get to find new subscribers for *DCA*. First I tour around the outside of the building, where I get to appreciate the juxtaposition of its peculiar architecture as it challenges and imposes itself on its neighboring structures. Then I go into the building and visit the atrium (all new buildings here have atria). After satisfying myself that I have gleaned as much as I could from this cursory visit, I move to the directory in the building lobby. There I go through the two dozen or so occupants and list those who might be future subscribers to *DCA*. Of course, I do keep an eye open for potential subscribers to my two other newsletters, but the bulk of subscribers to the other newsletters comes from direct mailing campaigns, which I will describe elsewhere. Having compiled my list, I then spend the next few minutes walking around the lobby, attempting to understand the architect's vision for this inner space. Also, as a one-time geologist, I note the finished stone and try to guess its source. This healthy diversion/excursion usually takes an hour or two, and I undertake it two or three times a month.

When I get back to my office in the National Press Building, I call information and ask for the telephone number of any one of the occupants I have listed, call the number, and ask the answering voice for the office's zip code; I have the address, of course. I then type out a number-ten envelope for each of the occupants I have listed, insert a *DCA* flyer and subscription form, paste on a stamp, and put it aside for mailing when I leave the building later that day. Over the years I've succeeded in getting something like a 6-percent hit rate for directed subscription solicitations of this sort. (I call it my lobby-hobby.) That's really very good; a direct-mail shotgun package usually brings in a 2 1/2 to 3 percent return.

My "lobbying" efforts have served also to acquaint me with other real-world Washington, D.C. phenomena as well. I've come to recognize the population of street vendors, street musicians, and street performers who congregate around downtown neighborhoods. And I see the homeless who, a block or two from the White House, flood Lafayette Park, and who warm themselves on the grates around the state department building—to all our shame.

24 | KEEPING SHARP

Honing skills, I

When you are working alone, always depending on yourself, it pays to keep your skills sharp, even in a trivial way. Set your mind to *expect* to always come out ahead, and most of the time you will. I decided to crash a sports bar, just to see if I could do it, surrounded as it was by very polite, but determined "hosts." After all, as an enterprising consultant, it becomes necessary, every now and then, to get past a determined gatekeeper-type-secretary to see the person in charge. Let's just call the sports bar escapade "practice" for the real thing.

I arrived in Atlanta, Georgia, on the Saturday marking the sixth game of the 1991 World Series. The plane at the next gate was filling with wild and wonderful Braves fans, their tom-toms pounding and tomahawks chopping, on their way to Minneapolis, where game six would be played. Really, I felt somewhat at home, because as an avid Washington Redskins fan I could appreciate temporary sports madness of this kind. I was in town (early, of course) for a professional society meeting I was chairing the following Monday, and had brought sufficient work with me to keep busy the entire weekend and then some. I hadn't counted (though I should have) on the Marriott Marquis Hotel being in a massive uproar at game time. There was nothing I could possibly do but join the loud crowd in the sports bar on the main level.

The hotel had filled a portion of its massive lobby with

59

TV monitors, and by game time there were several hundred guests splattered all around each monitor, wining and dining (mostly wining), and cheering on their Braves. When I squirted through to the sports bar, I was informed by a gatekeeper that they were filled to capacity, hence the overflow in the lobby. Well, a challenge is a challenge. I thanked him and turned away. Then, approaching from another angle, I spoke to a different guardian (I won't use the word "bouncer") these words before he could utter a sound: "Listen, I know you're full up, but I'm looking for a friend, and if he's not there I'll be out in less than thirty seconds, you can come and get me." So he let me in. I walked into the howling bedlam, with its giant TV screens, flowing alcohol, and screaming people and immediately headed back out. Close to the door a young lady asked if I expected to come back, and if so could she tattoo my hand with tonight's reentry stamp. Yes, I did, I said, and so she did what she said she would do. I was out in thirty seconds, waved to the original gatekeeper, and got lost in the mob out front. I then did a one-eighty, and came back in, showing the stamp on the back of my hand.

The game was enjoyable till the last of the eleventh, when Minnesota popped a homer. The home-team fans on TV went wild, while the Atlanta fans at the bar let out a mournful groan. I was feeling particularly miserable. The Redskins were playing the Giants the next night, and it was being broadcast nationally on ESPN. I had counted on seeing the game on these same huge screens. But with the Braves losing the sixth game of the series, every TV in the room would be tuned to game seven, and I would be all alone in my room, wearing my old Redskins T-shirt (the 'Skins always win when I wear that T-shirt—it was the first thing I packed for this trip) and cheering them on as they try to break the long-standing Meadowlands jinx. Wish us luck.

25 | DAWN PATROL

Amassing massive missives, and other early bird activities

I have always been an early riser, and I never have had trouble finding something to do with my time. Stated another way, I've always filled my plate, but never stopped looking for more. When I worked for the Environmental Protection Agency headquarters offices in Washington, D.C. I always arrived at work before 7:00 A.M. Again, this was not unusual for me. I have always found that the early morning hours have been my most productive, particularly since I am not then diverted by telephone calls, conversations, and coffee klotches. The one difference at EPA was that, for the first time in my working career, there was a fellow worker who always came in earlier than did I. But he did so for a very specific reason. And it wasn't for several weeks after my starting the job, until he got to know me and trust me, that he would share with me the reasons for his early arrivals. And it wasn't until months later that he allowed me to participate in his adventures.

I will hide his identity by referring to him as Joe. In truth, though he has long since retired from federal employ, and although he never did anything illegal or immoral (at least not in my presence and by my standards), I expect that he might be somewhat embarrassed if he recognized himself, by name, on any of these pages. What he did was to snoop. He was a prime snooper. He spent at least an hour every morning snooping. I say "at least" an hour, because I really don't know when Joe arrived at work. For all I know, he had a sleeping bag, razor, and change of clothes tucked away in the rabbit-warren of offices that make up the third floor of Waterside Mall, EPA's environmentally numbing headquarters shop. I do know that I never beat him to work.

Joe's job included the compilation of statistical data, anecdotal references, and accompanying documentation that formed the basis of EPA's regular enforcement reports to the public and Congress. However, he had discovered early on that the various EPA program offices around the building that received such information from the agency's laboratories and field offices were reluctant to pass those data on to him. I suspect the reason was because the responsible offices really weren't doing such a good job in pollution control and abatement, and they didn't want anybody to know, especially the public and Congress. Mind you, this was before passage of the Freedom of Information Act, and a good bureaucrat could easily hide his stack of paper from the prying eyes of outsiders. But nothing could keep Joe from his self-appointed rounds and from fulfilling the requirements of his own job description. Joe began to make his early-morning (and maybe even late-night) forays into wastebaskets, onto desk tops, around copying machines, and any other, as he called them, " . . . centers of accumulated paper." (Again, remember that this was the early seventies, and the personal computer, now a ubiquitous presence atop every bureaucrat's desk, did not yet exist.)

Well, every morning, Joe would appear with an armful of paper. Some of it was uncrumpled waste, some were copies he had made of original documents, some were copies of copies, some were no more than torn shreds of paper which apparently still contained items of interest. He would then walk into his office and compile all the material into a document he called the "daily dirt," lower cased d-d. Joe did very well for himself. He accumulated several civil service awards, and when he finally retired (I was by then at NASA), he left the building empty-handed, never looking back. The new occupant of his office, someone we both knew, told me years later in a chance meeting at a Christmas party that it had taken four janitors the better part of two working days to remove and dump the paper they had found in Joe's office.

But I've digressed a bit. My own participation as a "deputy snoop" in Joe's dawn sweeps was excellent training for me. Not that I ever engaged in such an activity on my own in the years that followed, you understand. I had always appreciated the concept of the "early bird getting the worm." But I didn't fully comprehend the significance of that phrase till I met Joe and shared some of his adventures and discoveries. Indeed, my own modifications to the apprenticeship I served at his side have led to a whole host of what I call "early actions." They are as diverse as could be, with the only common thread—be there first! Two examples are

(1) *Come early to the airport.* I always arrive at an airport at least an hour before scheduled departure. On business trips I usually fly coach. (In negotiations with a client I will "reluctantly" give in and accept coach tickets, but in turn insist on—and receive—business class for cross-country flights and first class for overseas travel.) Most airlines will hold the seats behind the bulkhead separating first class and coach for gate assignment, and a shade-side bulkhead window seat (opposite the sun side of the aircraft) is my seat of choice. If possible I reserve this seat on making my reservation; otherwise an early arrival usually assures me of this seat. Quite often, and depending on the length of the flight, the time aloft will provide you with a remarkably productive opportunity to undertake serious work. You will be comfortably seated and undisturbed. On every occasion I ask the agent to block off, if possible, the seat next to mine, informing the agent that I have much work to do and paper to spread around. If the flight is not expected to fill up, and most do not, I will be thus accommodated. Most airlines, though they board by seat number—last row first—will usually announce early boarding for families with children, first-class passengers, and passengers who feel they need a little extra time to board. I never qualify for the first two categories, but always take advantage of the

last. By boarding early I avoid the massive rush. But more important, I am assured of sufficient space in a now empty (but soon-to-be-filled) overhead compartment in which to stow my carry-on luggage. The worst thing to happen is to have no room in the overhead compartment at your seat row and watch the flight attendant take your carry-on luggage (a) to the rear of the plane and stow it in an empty bin at row 37 or so (try getting it when the plane lands) or (b) to the front of the plane, removed, and tucked into the belly as checked baggage (add an extra thirty to forty-five minutes to your destination).

(2) *Come early to a meeting.* If at all possible I make it my business to reconnoiter a meeting place that is new to me. If I am attending a meeting, meeting a client, or conducting an interview in a place I've never before seen, I try to look it over well ahead of time. I check the lighting (will I be able to see what I'm writing?). I estimate the direction from which the sun will shine (will it be in my eyes or his?). If we are meeting in a restaurant I determine the location of telephones, bathrooms, and exits (the three important destinations, so that I can head out to any of them with confidence). If I am picking up the tab I make certain that the maitre d' knows to inform the waiter, so that the bill is handed to me directly, rather than falling neutrally and awkwardly in the center of the table. In situations where I am to deliver a lecture I check the placement of the screen and the projection equipment and try out a few slides and viewgraphs to make certain that the equipment is working properly. Ditto the microphone and pointer. I always confirm a meeting a day in advance. This allows me to speak to an executive assistant, secretary, or receptionist beforehand. When I arrive early for the meeting, if it is held at the other person's office, I can address the gatekeeper by name, ask to see the conference room, and set up. I also use that opportunity to engage in as much small talk as possible, because you never know when you will pick up a vital piece of information that could be crucial in your upcoming meeting.

I know people who make it their business to arrive at an appointment exactly on time—not a second early or a second late. I also know people who take pride in always being late for every single thing they do. Though I understand the reasons for both, I am truly impressed by neither. What impresses me is the person who comes to any situation fully prepared—expecting and receiving no surprises. Joe 'n me. We were never surprised.

26 | ORNAMENTATION

Sending a message, II

I don't wear coats that often, and ties even less. But whenever I wear a coat or a tie, I do adorn each with a tiepin and/or lapel pin. I remember wearing tie clasps as a child when we were dressed up for special occasions. I stopped wearing them as soon as I could, and when I received a Texas tie clasp as a gift (recalled elsewhere), I realized I had not worn one in years. What I discovered, however, was that an ornamentation on your tie or on your coat lapel, can transmit a very specific message. It can say, "I am a member of the Snooty-Tooty Country Club" or "I work for MegaCorp, Inc." or "I am a Fellow of the National Academy of Aesthetic Agnostics" or something like that. Beyond simply making a statement, such ornamentation is also an icebreaker that quite clearly says, "Are *you* also a member?" or "Who do *you* work for?" or "To what professional status do *you* profess?"

Working alone, you must look for all means by which you can establish lines of communication to a person who might be a potential source of income. And a small, inexpensive accessory can often do the trick for you. In the past twenty-five years I have collected an incredible array of tiepins, tie tacks, tie clasps, and lapel pins. As a matter of principle I always purchase these from any social, technical, or professional organization that I join. But the majority of my collection has been obtained at yard sales and flea markets around the country. Some of them are quite impressive, both in terms of their visual appearance and the organizations they represent. I've never paid more than two dollars for any I've gotten this way.

If the occasion demands a coat and/or tie, I will always select an accessory that I would expect to be recognized at that particular gathering, and hopeful it would serve as icebreaker and conversation point. Granted, this may sound like a weak push forward, but never forget that working alone you must always look for any advantage, no matter how small, to facilitate discourse. And in our little world, the locomotive that travels from Discourse to Dialogue to Conversation to Exchange to Conference, often leads to Consultation. That's where the talk ends and the remuneration begins. I have often found that a little tiepin goes a long way in easing my train along that track.

27 THE LADIES OF LOCKHART, TEXAS

Know thy clients, lest you lose them

Within a geology department graduate student population exceeding one hundred, I was the only one working toward a degree in geological oceanography (or, more accurately, marine geology). In 1964 I was a doctoral candidate at the University of Texas at Austin. I had completed all my course work and had just returned from a one-year stint at the University of Southern California in Los Angeles, where I had undertaken my field work off the California coast aboard the USC research vessel *Velero IV*. The field of oceanography was just beginning to receive wide public attention, with marine geology getting its share of the spotlight—newspapers carried accounts of newly discovered findings in plate tectonics and continental drift. Austin, as the state capital, was always filled with legislators, many of whom were graduates of the university. One day the department chairman received a call from a state senator. He requested that a lecturer be sent to his hometown of Lockhart to deliver a talk on oceanography to the Women's Club of his fair city, his wife being chairlady of that august organization. The chairman pointed to me and said, "Go."

I was more than enthusiastic, and viewed this assignment, not as a chore, but as an opportunity. Having just returned from my oceanographic adventures and full of knowledge, I prepared a remarkably inappropriate lecture. In retrospect, it was far too technical, far too advanced, far too long, far too boring, and altogether too much for

my audience. (But at the time I didn't know that—I was
to learn that lesson in a very interesting manner.) Further
compounding my foolishness, I loaded up my VW beetle
with rocks, sand, and cores I had recovered during my
recent excursions off the California coast. I brought maps,
charts, books, reports, and about fifty 35mm color slides—
with projector and screen. I was a walking data dump.

Lockhart, at the time, was a quiet, central Texas town,
not very different from several hundred other towns spread
across the state from the pine forests of East Texas to the
Llano Estacado to the Guadalupe Mountains to the Gulf
Coast. The town square was dominated by an old two-story
brick building that housed the town library on the second
floor. That was where my lecture was to be held. The
temperature outside on that June day was a blistering 101
degrees, and even with the windows open, it must have
been close to 120 degrees in that second-story library (there
was no air conditioning, of course). There were six women
sitting in a semicircle of hard ladder-back chairs, chatting
quietly, as I entered. Scattered on a side table were the
remains of a just-completed luncheon and the few sheets
of paper that recorded the Women's Club business meeting
that had just ended. Actually I had to make several trips to
bring up all the goodies I had prepared for my talk.

When the room was finally set up, the senator's wife
presented me to her colleagues, and flattered me with a
fine introduction. My initial remarks took but a minute
or so, and I then darkened the room to begin my slide
show. No sooner had the first slide appeared than a soft
buzzing began in the chairs around me. Within a very few
minutes, every one of the ladies were fast asleep. And I
still think that those who weren't, just pretended that they
were. I stopped talking, and didn't know quite what to do.
Finally, when it became obvious that further input on my
part was unnecessary, I very quietly removed all my rocks
and maps and charts and other paraphernalia, and slipped
out of town.

One week later I received a very nice letter from the
state senator, copy to my department chairman, thanking

me for the talk I had given to his constituents in Lockhart, complimenting me on the quality of my demeanor and the knowledge I had exhibited. He was proud of the outstanding higher educational opportunities afforded by our state to its citizens, and would I please accept, as a small token of his appreciation, a sterling silver tie clasp bearing the seal of the State of Texas. Would I accept it? Of course I would accept it. I still wear it whenever I visit Austin.

The education I received that warm, embarrassing day in Lockhart has proved to be more vital and important to me than most formal courses I have taken, before or since. The specific lesson is a first principle for me and can be reiterated here in brief and in upper case letters: KNOW YOUR AUDIENCE. From the point of view of the client for whom you are working, and who is paying you:

(1) Define the task you are being paid to undertake, in terms of:
(a) a beginning point and (b) an end point;
(2) Lay out the path you will follow to get from (a) to (b);
(3) Move along that path with minimal exertion required for optimal result obtained; and
(4) Deliver an end product keyed to that client's expectations.

I have wondered many times how long it would have taken me to learn that vital lesson were it not for my meeting with the ladies of Lockhart, Texas, bless them all!

28 | THE GREAT POWER PUZZLE WAR, OR SHRDLU TO YOU, TOO

Honing skills, II

You can never be certain of tomorrow's weather, yesterday's memories, or who will end up sitting next to you on a crowded plane. When it is really impossible, for whatever reason, for me to work aloft, I will attempt to give into the natural sense of camaraderie, however ephemeral, that follows when two strangers meet as seat mates on an airplane. This is especially true if you are on the two-seat side and both of you are in a talk-and-listen mode. I must admit, though, that the best situation, at least for me, is a seat mate who is unknown and remains so throughout the flight. This is more difficult on a cross-country or international flight, because it becomes rather strained *not* to say anything for five or more hours. Generally, I bring sufficient work aboard with me, keyed to the length of the flight, to preclude all but cursory conversation.

Having noted the above, I also stress the fact that there will be notable exceptions, and I must admit to making some very interesting, and one very lucrative, contact aboard an airplane. Every now and then, however, I come across A Challenge. This is a gauntlet tossed my way by my seat mate. It usually comes in the form of a one-upmanship repartee that I am expected to lose. This is because my jeans and sweatshirt are not expected to stand up to the power suit guy or gal beside me. I usually win. But I want now to share with you an event that occurred last month, where I not only lost, but lost badly. The reason

71

I am relating this event at all is so that both you and I
will be suitably impressed with the sly cleverness of people
other than ourselves and we will remember that a top gun
always eventually meets a top-*per* gun. After reading this
I hope you'll still respect me . . .

On this particular flight I decided to use a first-class
upgrade that was about to expire. I selected the 1-A seat
on the shade side of a morning flight from Washington
National to Monroe County Airport in Rochester, New
York—flight time less than an hour. It was the beginning of the month, and that meant that the USAir in-
flight magazine would have a new crossword puzzle. I
love crossword puzzles, and take some pride in working
them in pen—finishing difficult ones more often than not.
I was first on board, and having deposited my carry-on
in the overhead compartment, I settled in my seat, pulled
out the magazine from the rack at my side, and began
working the crossword. A scant minute before departure,
1-B appeared. Well-appointed and well-dressed, he seemed
somewhat nonplussed at finding Mr. Bluejeans occupying
the window seat next to him. He was undoubtedly further
distressed to find the overhead filled and no room for his
own luggage. (DC-9s have notoriously tiny overhead com-
partments. I always check the aircraft type when making
my reservation, and if it is a "9" I make certain to board as
early as possible, just to forestall the possibility of ending
up like Mr. Flustered Powersuit, now glaring down at me.)
Well, I thought, tough. That's why I come early, Jack. But
he said nothing. The flight attendant found room for his
carry-on across the aisle. We spoke not a word to each
other during the entire flight. We were too busy engaged
in battle—word battle, that is. Upon noting the fact that I
had begun the crossword puzzle, in ink, and using a real-ink
Mont Blanc pen, no less, he immediately whipped out his
own Mont Blanc and began attacking the same puzzle in
his in-flight magazine.

As I glanced across, I could see that he was filling in
squares at a much faster rate than was I. It was positively
disheartening. I had obviously come across a world-class

expert. In fact, by the time we had initiated our descent into the Rochester area, he was finished with the puzzle, and with a resounding snap aimed in my direction, he closed the magazine and replaced it in the holder in front of him. I was barely two-thirds finished. Well, like I said, there's always someone just a bit faster, and one day you meet up with him. Of course, I did not admit defeat so easily. I even considered that he had already solved that particular puzzle on earlier flights. In truth, I had convinced myself that this was a fact as we taxied to our arrival gate. I was going to respond to the nasty smirk on his face by accusing him of just such perfidy, when I remembered, with total exasperation, that this was the beginning of a new month. That meant a new magazine, and a new crossword puzzle. Ah well, go down gracefully, I thought.

I don't know why I did it, but as the door opened and 1-B disappeared from view, I reached over, pulled out his magazine, and turned to the crossword puzzle page. Yep, every square was filled, neatly and in ink. However, I was startled to find that my competitive friend had simply spent the time putting in random letters in each square. One-across was M-I-Z-T-U; one-down was M-L-C-C-Q-M-H, and so on. I could only shake my head and smile. "Good on you, mate," I thought. You got me. But you didn't get me. But you think *I* think you got me. But you don't know I know you *didn't* get me. Get it? This all raced through my mind as I entered the Jetway at full speed. He was now several steps ahead of me, and although I couldn't see his face, I know he was still smirking. Well, I thought, should I say something or should I say nothing. It would be much more gracious for me to say nothing and simply bathe in the glow of silent victory. But as I passed him I saw myself lean over, and heard myself say out loud, "Good try, Jack, but one-across is M-I-Z-T-*O*, not M-I-Z-T-*U*." I kept walking and, son-of-a-gun, wouldn't you know it, *I* was smirking.

29 NEGOTIATING WITH THE PROSPECTIVE CLIENT

In this corner, wearing the Black Belt of knowledge, is the consultant . . .
and in that corner, wearing the Green Money Belt, is the prospective client. . . .

Professional negotiators, those individuals who make a serious living going around the country holding seminars on helping you to hone your negotiating skills, would be the first to note that all we do, *all we do,* in our lives is based on negotiations of one kind or another. This includes *all* aspects of our personal and professional lives. We all negotiate all the time. I believe this to be true. And if you, too, will accept that as true, then it should follow, should it not, that having spent scores of years fine-tuning our own negotiating skills, we all should be experts. We should be surrounded by a universe of *numero uno, top banana, el honcho grande, dai ichi ban honcho* negotiators—not so? But, unfortunately, we are not all so endowed. The sad end points of the negotiating-skills spectrum are peopled by

(1) the poor klutz who, when negotiating the purchase of a used car doesn't blink when the salesman rattles off an outrageous price, and then simply nods assent when the salesman adds, " . . . and the tires are an extra two hundred dollars," and agrees amiably when the salesman quickly adds, " . . . each"; and
(2) the bands of lawyers and politicians who, daily and as a matter of course, commit such atrocities as plea bargaining criminal cases and arranging S&L bailouts.

Most of us fall in between somewhere, drifting between the end points above. When you work alone you do not have the ability to carry out in-depth studies as to the multitude of rate schedules and fee structure options currently in vogue. Most everything I do as a consultant is geared to a financial return that I feel is large enough to satisfy me, yet not so high as to instill panic in the client's mind. I have elsewhere discussed specific per diem rates. But the most difficult assessment one must make is the size of the fiscal comfort blanket surrounding a prospective client.

In an initial discussion, most of the time is usually spent as a give-and-take, question-and-answer session. Here the prospective client is attempting to relate to you:

(1) what exactly he needs help doing,
(2) why he needs you to provide that help, and
(3) when he needs that help.

It is your job to

(1) affirm the fact that he needs help,
(2) attest to the fact that you are the person to help him, and
(3) confirm the fact that his time schedule coincides with your own availability.

Note that in this discussion there has been no overt reference, by either party, to a consulting fee or contract. If you are contacted by someone and the very first question he asks is your per diem rate, it is a safe bet that you have just encountered a small fry. Toss him back into the pond; you have no time to waste on him. The reason that you put off any serious discussion on your rate schedule is that as a consultant you do not have a bar-coded price tag attached to your brain. The general principle is that you will charge just about what you think the prospective client will pay. And there is no way to estimate his comfort range without engaging him in a discussion of his company's background and needs. Admittedly, while you are thus engaged, a part of your mind is concurrently inputting data into your embedded software program, "MacFee." And, having established the possibility, probability, or certainty of an actual consulting opportunity, the talk will undoubtedly soon move to the form and size of your expected remuneration.

Here it becomes serious. The prospective client, though not committing himself or his company to any course of action, has determined that he is interested in engaging your services, and asks you for a consulting rate. At this crucial juncture you must be ready to respond in a positive fashion. Your next answer can have only one of two results:

(1) It will be prelude to further discussion, or
(2) It will terminate the relationship.

Also, you alone have the option of foreclosing further discussion and terminating the relationship if you feel that

(1) the prospective client is proposing something illegal;
(2) the prospective client comes across as something less than honest;
(3) there would appear to be a conflict of interest, based on some other work you are doing, or
(4) for whatever reason your "hunch machine" rings up a "Just Say No!"

Many times—not often, but more times than you might expect—an initial meeting becomes a terminal meeting. In that case you shake hands and each of you goes his own way. But of course you would prefer this meeting to be but the first step of a long, enduring, and profitable relationship; which means that by the time you are asked your consulting rate, you have already fed in data such as his company size, company reputation, length of job, difficulty of job, prospect for continuing relationship, etc. into MacFee. The program printout, visible only to your mind's eye, has by now provided you with a pretty narrow range of fees. Taking that range into consideration, you must now use whatever skills you have accrued over the years to provide the prospective client with an acceptable verbal response.

It gets kind of sticky here. The professional negotiators I mentioned earlier all have different ideas, but the one thing they all seem to agree on is that the person who quotes a number first is the loser in any negotiation. Though I believe this to be true in most instances, there are categories of negotiation to which this general rule does *not* apply. A consulting negotiation happens to be one of those categories. I have never been able to accept a prospective client's number as an initial point of departure for serious negotiation of a per diem rate. From early experiences, where I did follow the advice of professionals, and maneuvered the fellow across from me to put his number on the table *first*, that number was invariably far below anything I could even begin to modify in a negotiated format. I was inevitably forced into either (1) coming back with a realistic (to me) figure that he felt was way out of line or (2) coming back with a somewhat higher figure that satisfied him, but left me very uncomfortable.

When I started building a client base I often took option (2). But what I am attempting to do for you now is to have you bypass that transition period and get right to where I am now. What I now do—what *you* should do—is to accept the range you have mentally calculated and quote a number from the higher portion of that range. You must also make the decision, *and stick to it,* so that if the ensuing negotiations lead the prospective client to demand a fee that is below the bottom of your range *you will turn down the job.* Granted, this is a serious move, but it is one that you must live with and stick with. I have, over the years, lost several jobs that way. I also have had occasions where the prospective client, having turned down my final number and terminated our discussion, called back the next day accepting my fee.

Even though you cannot know which way it will go, you must stick with your fee range numbers. You must treat a client with respect, and he must treat you with respect. You will receive from that client exactly the amount of respect that you demand. The very worst thing is for you to be hired on "cheap" in the eyes of the client. After all, your main job is to provide him with expert advice. His acceptance of that advice and any actions he pursues based on that advice must stem from a sense of continued, high, and demonstrated respect he has towards you. Anything less is unacceptable.

Remember also that as a consultant you spend your life very much as if you were at a bus stop. If you just missed your bus, there will always be another coming your way in a few minutes. Just never lose heart!

30 WASHINGTON REMOTE SENSING LETTER

Newsletters, I

I admit it. I was an unusual bureaucrat. I always felt that my employment as a Washington headquarters employee was more of a "means" than an "end." *Learning* was, and still is, a basic part of my being, and I viewed my years with the government in that light. I always felt that federal employment would provide me with an exceptional opportunity to meet new people and learn new things. I never expected nor did I desire a long-term, full, life-ending career—pension and all—with the Fed. I know that I make federal employment seem like a terminal disease, and to the many, many federal employees I know and respect, that can come across as an insult. I offer no apology, but merely ask you, my friends, to take pen and paper in hand and on the top center of the page, write, "Notable Career Accomplishments." Write one line per accomplishment. Please be honest (for instance, drafting a speech for the boss is not a notable accomplishment. Neither is attending an international conference—you know what I mean by a *notable* accomplishment). Now divide the number of lines written by the number of years you have been receiving government paychecks. That's the number of really important things you have accomplished per year of federal existence. Again, if you've been *really* honest in compiling your list, and suffer from high moral standards, you will now be in a funky mood for a few days. Following that mood, and then depending upon (1) your personality (2) how close to

(or how far from) a pension you are, (3) the state of the
economy, and (4) your personal life circumstances, you
will, like Kenny Rogers' *Gambler,* either (A) hold 'em,
(B) fold 'em, (C) walk away, or (D) run. I was a (B) (D)
person myself. Never intending to stay too long, and having
squeezed all that I could out of my government jobs at both
NASA and EPA, I folded and ran.

But one must, of course, have a plan of action before
undertaking such a drastic step. From the beginning, years
prior to my resignation from NASA, I had been aware
that most civil servants exhibit what I call an "Ensign
Pulver-like" mentality. You all remember the good ensign.
Superbly portrayed in the film version of *Mr. Roberts* by
Jack Lemmon, Pulver had served fourteen months as laun-
dry and morale officer aboard the small navy ship that
plied the backwaters of the South Pacific that was the
setting for the play and movie. In all that time, he had
managed to avoid the ship's captain. When they finally
do accidentally meet, the captain is astounded to learn
that Pulver has been aboard his ship all those months.
For most of that time, Pulver was stashed out below decks,
on his bunk, killing time and plotting (but never carrying
out) mischievous raids aimed at the captain, whom everybody hated. My comparison of Pulver to the typical civil
servant is astonishingly valid, or so I declare. The basic
theme for mid- to high-level managers in Washington, D.C.
agency headquarters is " . . . Make Ye No Waves, Lest
Ye Bring Down Thine Own Ship!" Doing what you are
told to do, no more and no less, very quickly becomes a
way of life. Translated, this also means Keep your nose
where it belongs; Don't dwell in other people's offices;
Don't learn about other people's projects; and Never participate in activities that stray from your own programmatic
responsibilities. All of these tenets were (and still are)
diametrically opposed to my own "order of battle." I go
through life with antennae extended. I live and love to
learn, and in the Fed that meant participating in as many
interoffice, interdivision, and interagency activities as possible. It meant organizing professional society symposia. It

meant meeting people, exchanging ideas, attending conferences, giving professional papers, accepting speaking engagements, and most of all, acquiring intelligence. All of the above—*all* of the above—are an anathema (if not a malediction) to the principles of a proper, cautious, career-conscious where-you-stand-depends-on-where-you-sit civil servant.

And let's not forget about the ram-jet principle. The ram-jet is a technologically simple device made up of an empty chamber into which fuel is injected, mixed with air, and ignited. The resulting explosion forces out an exhaust from the rear nozzle, which then propels the chamber (and the attached vehicle) forward. The point is that the higher the air/fuel concentration in the chamber, the greater is the explosion, and the faster the vehicle moves. Likewise, the faster the vehicle moves, the higher the air/fuel concentration, and the greater the explosion. Tongue-in-cheek-like defying the second law of thermodynamics, we say that, "The Faster it Goes, the Faster it Goes." And, like a ram-jet, so went my life as a civil servant. By spreading myself far and wide in the Washington bureaucracy I learned more and more about more and more. It was an exciting, exhilarating, and rewarding experience.

I had established a far-reaching network as well. Washington, D.C. offices (1) serve a transient population of temporary duty (TDY) federal personnel, (2) provide a training ground for federal interns and fellows, and (3) bring state, local, and private sector managers to Washington for a year or two via the Inter-Personnel Act (IPA) exchange agreement. I got to know as many of these as I could, and as all of them eventually scattered back from whence they came, they thus provided me with additional sources (and sinks) of data and information.

The Washington, D.C. federal headquarters' offices of all agencies and departments do serve as a permanent intellectual resource base, and I plugged into that system wherever possible. That infrastructure, here in Washington, D.C., serves as the most concentrated agglomeration of prime source materials in existence anywhere on this planet. And if you add to that the host of lobbying organizations, professional/technical societies, and countless ex-congressmen and senators who " . . . never went home again," you can begin to appreciate the extent and mass of the data bank here available. Further, I felt that I had alone, against odds, without support, and with sometimes active opposition from my peers and supervisors, amalgamated this data bank and fine-tuned its output to keep me continually updated on events dealing with my own fields of interest.

When it came time to leave the government, I knew that I wanted to work alone. After all, I had spent years in the Washington ocean visiting the various bureaucratic ports of call in my own little canoe. By that time I was convinced that I wanted no one above me and no one below me— unsupervised and unsupervising. I also knew that, using the network I had established, I wanted to do two things concurrently: (1) "rent my brain" to single customers for a high fee, as a consultant and (2) "rent my brain" to many subscribers for a low subscription rate, as a newsletter publisher. I considered both activities as complementary, symbiotic, and compatible. I planned to establish the consulting firm the day after I left the Fed, and I did just that. (Associated Technical Consultants is discussed elsewhere.) It took me somewhat longer to gear up for the newsletter activity, and that will form the basis for the remainder of the discussion below.

During my years in government I had not only been accumulating data and sources, I had also continually been "plowing back" into the system by providing data and information to my fellow workers. Though they were determined to "hunker down" in their own offices, many were really hungry for the kinds of activities in which I so openly and shamelessly engaged. And though they would not endanger their own careers by bucking the system, they had no problem in contacting me to learn details of events in our own and other agencies that might impact their own programs. During my last year at NASA, then, I was acting as both a two-way conduit and a central switchboard. And this would serve me exceedingly well as both a consultant and a newsletter publisher.

I left government employ in October 1980. My first efforts were directed towards consulting, and by December 1980 I had secured my first contract. It was with the Environmental Protection Agency, where I had worked five years earlier; I will describe the events leading up to that work elsewhere. By early 1981, I had ratcheted up my plans regarding the newsletter. All my efforts at NASA and the majority of my efforts at EPA had been directed to the various applications of satellite remote sensing. In plain English, I dealt with photographs of the earth derived from satellites that circled the globe. And specifically, I was interested in the host of *applications* of this imagery to diverse problems in such areas as (1) environmental monitoring, (2) crop yield and production estimates, (3) mineral and petroleum exploration, (4) coastal zone management, (5) land use planning, (6) forest inventory, (7) natural disaster assessment, and so on. My newsletter, then, would report on these activities, worldwide.

When I decided on the newsletter's content and coverage, I began to draft an initial flyer to advertise its coming existence. My goal was to have much of the paperwork in place by April 1981, to coincide with a scheduled national meeting on satellite remote sensing planned for Washington, D.C. at that time. I planned to distribute my flyers at that meeting. So from December 1980 to March 1981, off and on, I worked on all of the big and little details that it took to start a newsletter from scratch—alone. (Such audacity. I never, in all my years in college or since, had taken a course in journalism, business, accounting, or marketing. If I was to do things wrong—and I am told that I hardly did anything right—then at least I was happy. If ignorance is indeed bliss, then I was in a state of ecstasy!)

An early decision I had to make was the name of the newsletter. The words "remote sensing" had to appear, of course. I settled on "Washington" being part of the name, since at that time (and still today) Washington, D.C. was at the center of all activities dealing with satellite remote sensing. With the recent (post-1986) entry of the Europeans, Japanese, Russians, Canadians, Israelis, and other nations into this once all-American arena, the concentration of expertise and interest has indeed shifted somewhat. But the technological, budgetary, market, and programmatic axis is still centered in our nation's capital. I chose "Letter" instead of "Newsletter" because it provided me with license to use the informal writing style I enjoy. Hence, the *Washington Remote Sensing Letter* (*WRSL*) was conceived. Its gestation period was to be a scant six months.

The newsletter needed a home. What I was looking for was a prestigious address attached to a long-term lease. During my federal tenure I had often visited the National Press Building, and I always came away impressed with the facility and its occupant list. It is the home of not only the U.S. media, but the foreign media as well. As you travel the hallways of its twelve lower floors, reading the nameplates on the doors, you see represented dozens of major U.S. and international broadcast and print journalism organizations. Further, and more to the point, the perception that a potential subscriber would have as regards a newsletter published from the National Press Building would be invaluable. I suspected, however, that I might be shooting too high. Nonetheless, I decided to push ahead.

I began by visiting a gentleman I had run into during my earlier days at the Environmental Protection Agency. He was the publisher of a well-known environmental newsletter. His newsletter reported on all aspects of environmental concerns, and I always read it during my EPA days. I knew it was a successful venture, because by 1981 it was in continuous publication for at least ten years. I recall seeing the newsletter in several EPA offices, in industrial waiting rooms, and in libraries. I had no appointment with the editor, and planned simply to walk in, somehow get past his secretary, present myself as a neophyte newsletter publisher, and seek his advice. I hesitated a moment or two at his door, a bit unsure of myself. I was especially uncertain as to how to explain my determination to "go it alone" in the face of what was certain to be professional cynicism; my own perception of a newsletter operation was based solely on a combination of TV, movies, and fantasy. I expected to see a stack of reporters pounding away on Selectric IIs (remember, no PCs in 1981), screaming into telephones, and generally replicating a *Washington Post* newsroom on a Nixon resignation day. I pictured my newsletter editor friend *à la* Ben Bradlee, surrounded by his editorial staff, barking orders. After all, it does take an *organization* to run a successful newsletter operation, not so?

Not so. Imagine my surprise—then imagine my delight— at finding inside that newsletter office the following: one man (middle-aged), one telephone (black standard, rotary dial), and one typewriter (Underwood, manual). He greeted me warmly. I spoke and he listened, then he spoke and I listened. As I had hoped, there were no rules. There was some advice to be given and some advice to be taken, but no hard and fast rules. I left with the understanding that in the newsletter business you do what your gut tells you to do. And since I was ignorant of the different ways you *could* do things I would just proceed along, happily improvising as I went, and assuring myself that the way to go was the way I was going.

Now, one might claim that I would be spending a lot of time reinventing wheels. This is true. But the reinventor of wheels gets to learn a lot about the basic physics of wheel manufacturing, and I was to learn a lot about what makes a newsletter go 'round. And perhaps more important, by plunging ahead with some self-assurance, one finds no time to either bake in self-doubt nor baste in self-glory. You just do it. So I just did it.

I ultimately found the smallest office (with a window) that was available in the National Press Building. I began with month-to-month rental. (I have since gone to five-year leases, which allow for negotiating a lower dollar-per-square-foot rate). A good friend running a graphics studio in New York designed a *WRSL* logo for me, and

I had stationery and business cards printed. The National Press Building listed me, Murray Felsher, Ph.D., Publisher, *Washington Remote Sensing Letter*, Suite 1057-B, in the lobby directory. And a man came up and attached a signplate to my door saying the same thing. That same day I received from the Library of Congress an assigned ISSN, an internationally recognized numerical identifier for my newsletter. I was real. The newsletter, though barely conceived and still nonexistent, was nevertheless also real.

I next rented a Washington, D.C. post-office box in the city's main post office next to Union Station and applied for a Third Class Bulk Mailing Permit. The P.O. box would be my "fulfillment office" for subscriptions, with subscribers' checks, changes of address, renewals, etc. being sent there. The perception, again, would be of an organization somewhat larger than "one." Also, I felt that if, for any reason, I had to move from the National Press Building— like not being able to pay the rent—I wouldn't have to change all the flyers and forms citing the address to which subscription checks were to be sent.

I applied for membership to the National Press Club (NPC), which is located on the top two floors of the National Press Building. It provides outstanding opportunities to meet the newsmakers of the world as well as the news persons who report their doings. The NPC luncheons, televised live from the club's ballroom, have hosted nearly every global "name" one could imagine. Together with the "Newsmaker Breakfasts" and the countless press conferences held there, the NPC would allow this fledgling newsletter publisher to jump right into the middle of the big-news puddle. NPC concentrates the news sources in a geographically finite area, three floors above my office, and membership in the club would assure me of entree into this close-knit family of data gobblers. My membership card would also make it easier to obtain official press credentials from the U.S. Congress Periodical Gallery and (after a background security check) from the U.S. Department of State and the defense department. (As an aside, the DOD press conferences I attended at the Pentagon during Desert Shield/Desert Storm were a major learning experience for me.)

Well, I was slowly becoming a member of the press establishment. But Volume 1, Number 1 of the *Washington Remote Sensing Letter* was yet to be published. In fact, though I was internally confident of its eventual success, I had no outside assurances that such a venture was at all viable. There was no evidence that a newsletter specializing in my chosen topic would secure the sufficient subscribers necessary to pay the bills, much less the tuition of our oldest child, just then starting college. No similar newsletters were then in existence. Now this is worth a few extra words. I looked around and saw *no* newsletters, anywhere in the world, specializing in satellite remote sensing. In my ignorance I took this as a good sign. After all, here I was, first player on the field—what better way to stack the odds in your favor, right? Well, I was wrong again. I have since heard many wise heads in the newsletter business proclaim that if your type of newsletter doesn't exist, don't try to start one up. Conventional wisdom has it that either (1) it was already attempted and met with failure or (2) it's too dumb an idea to work.

I guess I was too ignorant to contemplate either of the above possibilities, because in April 1981 I walked over to the Washington Hilton, where a big meeting was taking place, and began distributing my *WRSL* flyers. The flyer itself was no work of art. I had composed it on my own typewriter; a single page of text with a subscription form at the bottom. The newsletter was advertised as a four-page monthly—I would not publish it at all in January and August, the months when Congress and the executive branch abandon Washington for more pleasant climes. I created a two-tier subscriber system with individuals paying one rate ($36) and institutions paying a higher rate ($54). These rates were for subscribers from the United States, Canada, and Mexico, and were to include first-class postage. Subscribers from all other countries were to pay $72, which included air mail delivery. The way that I had arrived at these subscription rates is worth a mention. I

visited the library at NASA headquarters, which I knew
carried a long list of newsletters, and discovered several
that were four-page monthlies. I took the highest rate I
found and added 20 percent. Yes, I know that was a weird
thing to do. Yes, I know I should have undertaken a total
market research effort, determined the universe of potential
subscribers, established a niche market segment, sent out
test issues, determined my full cost of doing business, calculated my expected return on investment, and back-filled
a subscription rate. But like I said, I was (and still am, to
a great degree) happily dumb.

So April 1981 found me with an armful of flyers in the
Washington Hilton. I got to the hotel early and set the flyers
all around the meeting rooms. When I noticed a meeting
official removing a stack, I'd follow him around, retrieve
the flyers from the trash, and replace them. Eventually he
got tired and left the field. I pasted the flyers up on pillars
and tacked them to walls. I handed them out to strangers
and friends. As time went on I would learn to pull out
my press credentials and seek permission from conference
officials to display and distribute my literature; they now
invariably agree to let me do so. At that first meeting,
though, I felt it was easier to beg forgiveness then to seek
permission. In the end I must admit to pangs of dismay
as I saw my flyers fly away in crumpled wads or, even
worse, lay ignored in ignoble piles. I couldn't help but
wonder if any would be read, or having been read, would
anyone subscribe.

The day following the end of the meeting I began haunt-
ing my P.O. box. It was a Thursday, and the box was
empty. Friday and Saturday, no responses. I was certain
there would be a letter or two in the box on Monday. Nope.
I visited the box daily. When Friday rolled around and I had
found the box empty all week, I admit that I was somewhat
confounded. But you must know that I was still several
acres away from "nervous," and a whole universe away
from "panic." After all, the ATC consulting activity was
moving along well, and there really was no danger of starv-
ing. The absolute worst thing that could happen was that

nobody would want to subscribe to a newsletter that dealt with remote sensing. Big deal! The world wouldn't end. At worst I would have lost some dollars and some time.

At any rate, two and a half weeks later, when I was expecting nothing (isn't it always like that?), a subscription order, along with a $36 check was innocently waiting for me in the P.O. box. I still remember it. It was from a scientist at NASA's Goddard Space Flight Center in Greenbelt, Maryland. The next day there were five orders. By the end of the week there were thirty-five subscribers. I was in business. It was a little business, granted. But now that I was certain the market was there I would work to make the little business a big business. Volume 1, Number 1 was published in July 1981, and we have been publishing *Washington Remote Sensing Letter* continuously since then. I still make up the rules as I go along, and instead of a typewriter I'm armed with a MacIntosh II, laser printer, fax, and modem. But I'm still doing it alone, and somewhere between then and now it's turned into a big business.

31 | MID-COURSE CORRECTIONS

Newsletters, II

By the time the first issue of *WRSL* was to appear, I had used my third-class bulk permit to mail out several thousand flyers, and had secured a considerably large readership, both domestic and foreign. Of course this considerably large readership was not yet reading anything, since I was not yet writing anything. When Volume 1, Number 1 was published in July 1981, I was fully confident that the newsletter would indeed succeed. Again, this was a rash statement to make. I have since been told—and straight-faced tell others—that you can't be certain of the long-term success of a newsletter until you have survived three renewal cycles. It's that old conventional wisdom, once more. Yet I knew, as I mailed out the first issue of the newsletter, that we had a winner. That first issue was typed on a Smith-Corona electric typewriter. It took me a total of fourteen hours to put it together. I brought the typed copy to a printer, who had already prepared 11″ × 17″ ivory 60-lb sheets to my specs, including logo and masthead in blue. The items I had gathered were newsworthy, though not spectacular. Included though, was a particularly interesting item I had obtained from a NASA friend. It related to a "tethered" magnetometer. It was to be an Italian-built instrument that would measure the earth's magnetic field. It would literally "hang" out of a space shuttle payload bay, attached to the shuttle by a kilometer-long string, or tether. I had sent my initial newsletter to the *Washington*

Post, Attn: Science Desk. (There actually was no science desk at the *WP*, but I didn't know that.) Lo and behold, two days later there was an item in the *Post,* citing the tether, and more important, quoting the *Washington Remote Sensing Letter* by name. For the next week my P.O. box near Union Station was filled with subscriber inquiries and checks.

Hmmm, I thought. So this is how it works. The more you know, the more you're known. The more you're known, the more people will pay to know what you know. The more people will pay to know what you know, the more opportunity you have to know more. And the more you know, the more you're known. . . . It's that 'ole ram-jet again; the faster it goes, the faster it goes.

And in that context, I had opted for a monthly newsletter even though, in my heart-of-hearts, I knew that publishing every month was getting the word out too slowly. It would quickly place my readership too far behind the power curve. Too much was happening in our remote sensing world, and I planned to move, as soon as possible, to a semimonthly format instead. Note that I said a *semimonthly* not a *biweekly* format. Okay. Time for a pop quiz. Now why would I opt for a semimonthly, which is two times per month, instead of a biweekly, which is every two weeks? Go ahead, think about it. I'll be back in a minute. . . . Well? Yes, you're right. I guess you're catching on after all. *Of course,* a semimonthly commits you to 24 issues per year, and a biweekly obligates you to 26 issues per year. But you knew that, didn't you? As it turned out I waited a year, then informed my readers that I was changing from a monthly to semimonthly format three months hence. I would publish *WRSL* twice a month, except January and August, when I would publish once a month. This brought us to 22 issues per year, which I felt I could easily handle. By that time I was receiving more information than I could use, and my biggest task was (and still is) culling rather than gathering. Type time per issue was down to seven to eight hours (still on my Smith-Corona).

I promised all of my readers that they would have their original monthly subscription periods honored, at no additional charge, for the semimonthly change. So they would receive *WRSL* twice a month for the run of their original once-a-month subscriptions. Of course I had to increase the subscription rate, and with a huge sigh and a bit of trepidation I did the following: (1) I eliminated the two-tier individual/institutional system, and went to a simple domestic (U.S./Canada/Mexico))/overseas (all other countries) basis; (2) I increased the domestic subscription rate from $36 (individual) and $54 (institutional) to $210 (Yes, $210!); and (3) increased the overseas subscription rate from $72 to $300 (Yes, $300!). There is no secret as to how I arrived at the new rates. I simply made them up out of whole cloth. By that time I had already gotten a good handle on my actual costs (rent, telephone, printing, postage, etc.) and I knew that I was operating deeply in the black as it was. By doubling my output and doubling my subscription rates, I knew I would do very well, simply by saving on economies of scale (in terms of paper and printing costs). Instead of doubling or even tripling the original average domestic rate, I about quintupled it to $210. Then I nearly tripled the overseas rate to $300. I can give you no economic or logical reason, explanation, or rationalization for my selecting those dollar figures—they just looked right to me.

I knew, however, that I would be losing many subscribers, especially those individuals who were paying for the subscriptions out of their own pockets. As to institutional subscriptions, as libraries, government agencies, and such, they are a different beast entirely. I stand convinced that "once is about forever," as far as those noble entities are concerned. Absent the most severe economic times, an institutional subscription once entered, is eternal in aspect. At least, that's what I decided. It *was* a gamble, true. I expected to lose at least half of my individual subscribers; I lost more than 70 percent of them. I expected to lose no more than 20 percent of my institutional subscribers; I lost less than 10 percent. As a matter of fact, during the following year there was an upsurge in subscriptions from institutions where many of the "lost" individual subscribers were employed. Evidently, either (1) individuals who could no longer afford to subscribe had convinced their libraries or supervisors to pick up the subscription or (2) their libraries had been paying for their subscriptions all along, but had opted to route payment through the individual in order to receive the lower rate ($36 versus $54). (That shows you what a true cynic I really am.) And by the way, that really was the major reason I had dropped the two-tier domestic structure—I had always felt that I was being snookered. Hey, I would have done the same.

About four years ago, citing increased postal and printing costs, I again increased my subscription rates. But this time the increase was not associated with any change in publication frequency. We still publish *WRSL* twenty-two times a year (twice a month, except once in January and once in August). But the rates went to $310 domestic and $400 overseas. And in January 1994, citing increased postage and printing costs, we increased rates again to $410 domestic and $500 overseas!

32 | CONFLICT OF INTEREST

Be discreet or meet the street

Conflict of interest. The three dreaded words!

In my consulting business I offer to provide an Operational Update (OU), which is a one-day briefing designed to bring a client up to speed on contemporary activities in a particular subject area. The briefing covers specific topics that have current and immediate impact on the client's business. I charge my very highest fee for one of these sessions. And though it is usually safe to assume that the client will know far less than you about a subject area, this is one instance when the client may indeed be very knowledgeable and sophisticated. As a result I approach my OUs with some caution.

I have discovered that I am sometimes brought in under these circumstances to spill some beans that I always keep locked up tight. On these occasions the client spends more time questioning me than I do briefing him. And the questions invariably rotate about what I call the P-cubed axis—that is, Personnel, Policy, and Programs. I have no problem whatsoever discussing my P-cubed perceptions as they relate to government agencies or companies with which I have no dealings. But often, a client will be more interested in those matters as they relate to another private sector company, usually a current or prospective competitor; many times that other company is also a client of mine.

Any consulting contract you sign will include a non-disclosure statement (NDS), which protects both you and the client. I will spend some time discussing the NDS elsewhere. Suffice it to say that I make it a practice not to acknowledge any contractual relationship I have with corporate client A when I am meeting with corporate client B. In initial discussions with B, which led to a consulting agreement, I had considered and dismissed any real or apparent conflict of interest between my current work with A and my upcoming work with B. Indeed, if there *was* a perceived conflict, I would not have agreed to work with B. Yet, it is very possible that, in the midst of an OU for B, I am asked to consider the outcome, say, of B responding to a government Request For Proposal (RFP) for which I know A is also responding, a proposal that I am actually helping A to write! And suppose B asks me to evaluate his chances as opposed to A. You see what I mean? It gets kind of difficult here.

My solution to this dilemma follows: If client B creates a condition that places me in a conflict of interest situation, then I must immediately terminate my work with B in favor of my prior commitment to A. At the same time, I am obliged, by my NDS clause with B not to inform A of any discussions I have undertaken with B. It's as simple as that. (Of course I will submit a prorated bill to B, covering the time I spent with him.)

The danger is imminent and real. Your very existence as a consultant is in no greater jeopardy than when you flirt with a conflict of interest situation. The best recommendation a consultant can have is to know that the community considers him trustworthy. The worst thing that you can say about a consultant is that he is "unreliable."

In my own travels around the Capital Beltway, I know that I am preceded, accompanied, and followed by the one factor that most critically affects my success, it's called my good reputation. And I guard it jealously.

33 | A FAR-EAST TALE

Quiet waters sometimes understand more than you think

The following little anecdote is of an event that occurred during my last year at NASA. My remembering every detail after all these years indicates the great impression it made on my psyche, and the lesson it taught me is even more important today than it was back then.

Our associate administrator, the man in charge of NASA's applications program and my boss, gathered together five of us technical people to meet a visiting delegation of five scientists from the People's Republic of China. We met in a second-floor conference room at NASA headquarters on Independence Avenue, just across from the still-new National Air and Space Museum. The Chinese visitors, all earth scientists—geologists and geophysicists—were accompanied by a translator from our own state department, who was shepherding them around the country. The purpose of their visit to NASA was to learn about our new earth-viewing sensor, called the Thematic Mapper (TM), that was to fly on a civilian Landsat satellite in 1982. The Chinese, with the concurrence of our state department, wanted to build a ground station that could down-link the TM imagery and thereby secure for themselves photography of the Asian mainland and surrounding territory.

The instructions from our boss were to cooperate with the state department and provide to the Chinese delegation a full technical briefing of the TM, its applications, and the ground station requirements. I wasn't certain what benefits *we* (the U.S.) would derive from this activity. And following assurances from Mr. State Department that his charges didn't understand any English (he'd been with them for a week by then, touring government technical centers), I engaged in a short discussion as to exactly *why* we were, to use the slightly inappropriate phrase, "unbuttoning our kimonos for these folks." The official response went on for five minutes, but a quick summary went something like this: Don't meddle with me. I represent the Department of State. I fly so high in government circles that you will get mental nosebleeds just *thinking* of the people I deal with. So just do what you're told to do, period (sneer).

Quid pro quo aside, then, we proceeded with our briefing. It went very slowly, because everything we said had to be translated from our technical English into technical Chinese by Mr. State Department. My perception was that our translator, though probably up to the job insofar as state dinners and protocol were concerned, he was falling far short and having a rough time getting the technical words across to our esteemed visitors.

I should also point out here that the five Chinese earth scientists were introduced to us as directors of the five most prestigious earth science institutes in the People's Republic of China, so they certainly were technically competent. But it was obvious that they were getting as frustrated with the translation process as were we. For the better part of an hour the NASA side (who spoke no Chinese) struggled along in their attempt to make the several technical points that needed making. All the while we were making side comments, and asking each other aloud, for the benefit of our translator, just why we were providing this briefing, and just what advantages the Chinese would derive from it. Finally beaten down, our translator responded (in English, of course) to our side-bar hammering. He confessed to us, in between technical translations for our guests, that he was not too sure himself why we were doing all this. He had already sat through half a dozen technical briefings for these gentlemen during the past week at U.S. facilities around the country, and he himself was convinced that they were neither technically sophisticated nor scientifically competent enough to understand even a smidgen of what they were being shown.

Finally, after a particularly complicated (but important) viewgraph filled the screen, our translator threw up his hands and said we'd just have to skip that one, as he couldn't begin to translate it. Then an amazing thing happened. One of the Chinese, the youngest of the "gang of five" said, very clearly and in colloquial English, "No. This is critical; let's go through it. Better let me handle it." And he did. Perfectly at ease, and with authority, he covered the viewgraph's salient points. He did so in Chinese, though sprinkled with enough English to let us know that his four colleagues understood every word of our earlier, *inter alia* discussions. He then, after seeking permission, reached over and pulled out several of the earlier viewgraphs, portions of which had been skipped. Again, he went over them in detail for his colleagues. We finished the briefing shortly after that, we speaking English and they understanding full-to-the-brim, highly technical data. If we NASA folk were astonished and amazed by this event, then our Mr. State Department was shocked and outraged. I still wonder what intelligence those five gentlemen took home with them.

As for me, there was driven and forever embedded into my brain a little sign that says: Assume He Knows; I filed it under Priority Folder One (PFO). When I meet someone for the first time, and we play the game of evaluating each other—in any situation, business or social—I drag my mental mouse to PFO and click open "Assume He Knows." Maybe he doesn't. No harm done. But maybe he does. And as a consultant, you never, ever, want to place yourself in a situation where you have underestimated the competence and knowledge of anyone across the table from you, especially if he claims no competence and little knowledge. Beware the quiet ones!

34 | MUXING TO THE MAX

Funda-mentals

In stark dictionary-ese, *multiplexing* is usually defined as the transmission/reception of several messages simultaneously on the same circuit or channel. In NASA-ese the three-syllable "multiplex" was shortened to a simple "mux," and changed from a noun to a verb, as in "We can do a workaround by muxing the warm bodies from all three projects in real-time." (In those days NASA could do *anything*, and by the way, a translation of the above is available by request.)

I never really appreciated the nuances of muxing until I left NASA. In essence, when you work alone you must have the appropriate combination of natural ability, mental agility, serendipity, and just plain good sense to continually receive and integrate data across the whole spectrum of subjects you are then engaged in; and you must do so in a concurrent fashion. If you are the kind of person who has a sign up on his wall that says, "Do only one thing at a time. Do it as long as it takes until you are finished. Put it aside and never think of it again, then move on to something else," then stay where you are. Keep your day job. In fact, put this book down—I don't know why you wasted your money. (Perhaps if it's not too dog-eared you can get a refund.) If you contemplate working alone, then you must already possess (or be willing to somehow acquire) an internal mechanism that is able to recognize and emplace correct portions of the incoming information bitstream into a recognizable and recallable relational data base. And that incoming bitstream may or may not carry a directional label that will facilitate its proper categorization.

For most people, not one piece of the above is a comfortable and instinctive mode of operation. When we are involved in the creative manipulation of a mental product, and the transfer of that product onto paper, we are usually engaged in this activity to the total exclusion of all else. Oh, a radio may be playing in the background or a clock may be ticking nearby, but the primary brain cells that are dealing with the matter at hand are clicked up to a "priority-one" setting, and everything else is trimmed back to "dormant/temporary." Neural synapses are crackling and nerve impulses are zapping along axons. The brain is chugging across the single track you are constructing.

Now suddenly, unbidden and without warning, a new piece of seemingly extraneous and irrelevant data breaks through "priority-one"; or perhaps a newly integrated information stack bubbles up out of "dormant/temporary." What happens next? What happens next will go far in letting you know if you are ready to take on the world alone:

(1) *What Happens Next is* if you are strong-willed and single-minded, and you have that sign up on your wall, and if you have to struggle to maintain a semblance of creative fluidity, you will then recognize and immediately resent the attempt of an exotic idea to establish a beachhead in your mind. You will defend the integrity of that prosaic coastline, and fortifying whatever weak points you may find, you will unhesitatingly slam the door shut on any distracting factors. Your train of thought will indeed keep chugging along that original single track. In so doing, you may have saved your original pristine thoughts and ideas, but at what cost! Innovation, spontaneity, diversity—all are gone. You have demonstrated an inability to receive and transmit more than a single item per channel. You are, to coin a phrase, "muxless"; (2) *What Happens Next is* you step back, startled. Interloping ideas come storming, unwelcome, through the door. They are uninvited and unwanted, but you are powerless to prevent their entry. They mingle, raw and

unimpeded, in among your earlier creative attempts. Words and ideas grow more discordant and conflicting. Confusion builds into panic. And your mind's hard disk crashes! I call this "mental white-out." You can recognize that it has happened to you when you suddenly realize that you've spent the last fifteen minutes staring at a semicolon on your computer screen. Again, your response indicates an inability, or unwillingness, to cope with the random addition of data and the tasks associated with integrating that data. You are muxless; (3) *What Happens Next is* you recognize the new ideas gaining entry to your mind as potential sources of creative inspiration. You open the door and let each in slowly, rounding off its edges. You step back and let the new ideas interact with your current thoughts. You free-associate, letting words and numbers, concepts and colors, fantasies and facts, all mingle and bounce off whatever happens to be darting about your frontal lobes at the time. And the result, invariably, will be more creative, more instructive, and more innovative than the original piece on which you were working. The whole will become greater than the sum of its parts, and you'll be "muxing to the max."

Most professionals, perhaps because they are quite literally surrounded by coworkers and *not* alone, feel they must confine their work habits, especially their cognitive procedures, to traditional, acceptable methodologies. Out of fear, embarrassment, or a combination of both, their written output rarely strays from the unimaginative, bland, well-beaten path. And perhaps those of us who literally *do* work alone feel more comfortable stepping, Frost-like, onto a road " . . . less traveled by . . ." If you are contemplating joining me on that road, more grassy and wanting wear, rest assured there is ample room for us both.

35 | A DAY IN THE LIFE OF A CONSULTANT

How do I charge thee? Let me count the days . . .

When you are working alone, "time" is both your greatest ally and your worst enemy, mainly because you never seem to have enough of it to do all the things you want to do. In its friendly garb, time is your basic work unit. You usually charge a per diem, or daily fee, and the more days you work, the more fee you receive.

I always negotiate my consulting agreements to include the phrase:

" . . . For billing purposes full days are eight hours and half-days are four hours; and the consultant will receive his specified per diem fee for each eight-hour day worked; partial days worked less than eight hours are increased to the next higher half-day."

This is a critical contractual insert. If you do not specify precisely what it is you mean by a "day," you are in effect giving the client the option to define it as any 24-hour period. This means that if you work from, say, 8:00 A.M. to 6:00 P.M., with a 30-minute lunch break, and then from 7:00 P.M. to 10:00 P.M. (as I have done on many occasions), you are then permitting the client to demand an invoice from you for only a day's work. Actually, you have put in 12 1/2-hours' work. In my book that's 8 hours (one day), plus 4 half hours. My contract considers the 4 half hours as a partial day, and raising that to the next higher half-day brings it to a billable one day. Total invoice submitted to the client would then be for *two* days' work, not *one* day's work. Q.E.D.

36 | AS TIME GOES BY

When time flies, so does your fee

I am often asked by my nonconsultant friends whether I bill the client at my regular per diem rate for travel time. That is, if I'm flying, say, from Washington, D.C. to San Francisco and back on a job, would I bill the ten-hour round-trip flight time. The answer is, "Yes." I have *never* been asked that question by a client. He understands that my daily billing rate is averaged and takes into account everything that I am myself charged (from postage to printing, from office rent to car costs) plus a reasonable profit above those expenses incurred. The per diem, taken over time, amortizes my cost of doing business, and the fee provides a residual profit. When I am working for a client I am being paid for the *time* I am in his employ (no matter what I am actually doing). I cannot be working and earning a fee from anyone else during that time. My rate is the same for those periods of time, whether I'm engaged in a highly technical discussion with his engineering staff, whether I'm getting a briefing from his marketing vice-president, whether I'm compiling a set of numbers for a final report, whether I'm sharpening a pencil, or whether I'm hurtling through the lower atmosphere at 500 miles per hour, snoozing.

37 CONSULTANTS DO IT FOR A FEE

The sounds of silent resentment

If you are fortunate enough to secure a lucrative, long-term contract with a client, you are apt to enter a somewhat different world—one not usually encountered even by the most experienced consultant working alone. Often, a *large* consulting firm will serve as a "body shop" for a federal agency or a large corporation. By this term we mean that the consulting firm is contracted to provide a substantial administrative service, like bookkeeping or program management or human resources, for that larger entity. In those cases, anywhere from several tens to several thousands of "warm bodies" are hired on by the consulting firm, which then pays these individuals through funding provided by the federal government or the large corporation. These individuals are not considered employees of that federal agency or large corporation, and receive no benefits (health plan, vacation, profit sharing, etc.) other than those that might be provided by the consulting firm itself. Though they work side by side with the "true" employees, the warm bodies serve only "as needed" and are terminated at will. (That is the main reason body shops are contracted; and they are contracted to satisfy either of two events: (1) to fulfill a particular contract for which the incumbent has no in-house expertise or (2) to serve as short-term plugs for financially leaking organizations.)

In rare instances, though, a lone consultant can find himself in a "body shop" situation. Despite his very high per diem, he may possess the talent and/or knowledge that is deemed so vital to the client's ultimate business success, that he is asked to stay on as a long-term consultant. Though the financial advantages of such an arrangement to a consultant are fairly obvious and do deserve some discussion, I want, instead, to concentrate on a somewhat insidious and hidden danger associated with such a situation.

A personal example: I once helped a corporate official traverse the intrapreneurial process within his own Fortune-fifty corporation that resulted in his being provided the necessary seed money and a new 45,000-square-foot facility to start his own corporate subsidiary, of which he was named president and general manager. The due-diligence procedures, including the various hoops we leapt through and gates we passed through, took a year and a half. In the two years following its creation, the subsidiary he formed went from zero employees (I didn't count—I was only a consultant) to 62 employees. My own participation in the subsidiary's incubation process was well recognized and well rewarded; all told I spent a total of five years as a long-term consultant for the parent corporation, averaging twelve invoice days per month. (In fact, I still provide operational update briefings for officers of the parent company.) My own work with the subsidiary was directed outward, and I was largely responsible for the early win of a one-million-dollar government contract (I say this factually; there is no arrogance intended).

As each new early employee was hired for the subsidiary, there was no lack of gratitude toward me, since it was understood that if I had not helped form the company, there would be no employees, period, and they would have no jobs. However, as more and more employees were hired, a growing animosity was directed at me by various company officers, which hinged on the fee I was receiving monthly. Although I had no benefits, did not participate in the employee ownership program, and drove no company car with cellular telephone, my consulting fee resulted in a monthly payment that was higher than anyone in the building, including the president and general manager. But that's why I'm in the business I'm in. That's what makes working alone great.

What followed, on the part of most of the sixty-two employees, was a tangibly real and growing resentment. It was strongest at the highest levels of the organization, wherein I spent most of my time when in the building, and although it decreased down the organizational ladder, it was still perceptible at the bottom rungs. For a salaried employee, be he an hourly mule on the loading dock or a "suit" with a key to the executive washroom, it became too easy to look at a highly paid consultant— perhaps with a strange mix of envy and jealousy, and feel both threatened and intimidated by his very knowledge and talent that brought the company to the position that it occupied. I found this a strangely interesting situation, as I had never experienced it before. I was careful, on my part, not to antagonize anyone, but to no avail. Though I was, in every sense, the ultimate insider, I began to be treated as an untrusted outsider. The issue played itself out with some fascination. As time went on, my own comfort index began to decrease. Then for other reasons, in the following rapid order, (1) the president was fired, and (2) the company closed its doors, and sixty-two employees were out on the street. In between (1) and (2), I got into my Corvette and drove away. If knowing now what I didn't know then, would I still take on a long-term, highly-paid consulting assignment and accept the inevitable animosity and resentment? You bet I would! And I would be glum all the way to the bank.

38 | THE SPOTTER-SCOPE SYNDROME

His mouth says "Yes," but his mind says "No"

Somebody once said that people who expect nothing are rarely disappointed. I never fully understood what that meant, because to me it could mean one of two things. It could mean (1), people who expect nothing *get* nothing, so they get what they expect, i.e., nothing. Ergo, they are rarely disappointed. Or it could mean (2), people who get *something*, after having expected nothing, are that far ahead of the game, and so are rarely disappointed. I believe that, working alone, you must always, *at a minimum*, operate in a case (2) mode. You must, *at least*, *expect* some success, and pursue that expectation actively. Most people, unfortunately, conduct themselves as in case (1) above, and as a result " . . . lead lives of quiet desperation."

My hope is that you will be able to move beyond "expecting nothing" to being prepared, motivated, and ready to respond to and take advantage of *success*. The mere assumption of success, though appearing to be a trivial and pedestrian attribute, is anything but that. With the certainty and knowledge of expected and eventual success comes a willingness and eagerness to embrace and enlarge upon those results. Failure begets failure, success begets success. It's as simple, and as complex, as that.

It is essential, however, to understand that "success" is an end that cannot be reached passively or inertly. In general, you cannot lay back and allow events to unfold. Instead, you must be a prime mover in those events which define your own interests. Along with that realization, for anyone hoping to succeed working alone, is what I call the "principle of dependency." By that I mean a bit more than the often stated, "you alone are responsible for your own destiny." It is far too passive a statement for me, and requires some expansion. I would have you believe that not only must you depend, to the greatest extent possible, upon yourself, you must also depend, to the least extent possible, upon others.

Lest this be interpreted as a cynical and antisocial remark, let me at once emphasize that I am writing this book to communicate to you, the reader, a mind-set amenable to your pursuing a career, and making a very good living, by working alone. I can neither demand, nor insist on philosophical congruence between us. However, I can assure you that minimum dependence on others, in the workplace, is both professionally stimulating and profitable. This might seem a difficult point of view to accept, especially in these days of group dynamics, teaming, joint problem-solving, and all the other cute and cultist exercises being undertaken by corporate America in its slide down the competitive flagpole. These examples of mutual dependency, as vital as they are to the survival of the weakest links in an organizational chain, are an anathema to anyone working alone.

To the greatest extent possible then, I depend upon myself in the workplace. To the least extent possible then, I depend upon others. I actively press against the envelope of my expectations, and actively move events in a manner designed to accomplish a sought-after goal in expectation of success. If you happen to have been born with these personality characteristics, I envy you. I was not. As for me, I had to learn the hard way—but once learned, always remembered!

It happened when I was attending graduate school in Massachusetts. I had planned a summer's work on my master's thesis studying the Cape Cod beaches, (don't laugh, we call it coastal morphology and sedimentology). I needed a spotter-scope to set up on the berm crests to estimate wave heights at different distances offshore. The only spotter-scopes available were under the control of the university's

R.O.T.C. unit, where they were used to mark shots at the rifle range. Since this was July, and the cadets were not in residence during the summer, I was certain that I would be allowed to sign out a scope for a few weeks. Indeed, when I spoke to the army major who was the deputy commander of the R.O.T.C. unit, he was kind and attentive. He also seemed interested in my work, and we spent thirty minutes discussing such beach characteristics as soil moisture and trafficability as they applied to amphibious landings (okay, I was buttering him up). His last words to me as I was going out his door were for me to tell his supply sergeant down the hall that he, the major, had no problem with my signing out a spotter-scope immediately. I left, feeling pretty good, and hadn't gone more than a few feet when I realized that I hadn't thanked him for his efforts on my behalf. So I wheeled around and opened his door, just in time to hear him tell his supply sergeant on the phone, " . . . and under no circumstances will you allow him to sign out a spotter-scope—think up any excuse"; at which point he looked up and saw me standing at the open door. He looked surprised, but not dismayed, and certainly not embarrassed. After a moment he simply shrugged his shoulders slightly, as if to say, " . . . and that's the way it goes, sonny," and went about his work, ignoring me completely.

I don't know how long I stood there, but it was for whatever length of time it took my emotions to run the gamut from stunned to outraged. I left without saying anything, and returned to my desk in the graduate student's "bullpen." True, I was young and had a lot to learn—and what I learned that day I carry with me still. You see, I had two choices; either I could let the matter drop or I could actively pursue it; it was as simple as that. The initial response to such a situation could have been, from that day forward, not to believe anyone. Trust nobody. Instead, I decided to consider the event from the major's point of view. He didn't want me to have the spotter-scope, yet he didn't want to confront me with that fact. Instead, he chose to play an end game that, in essence, sacrificed the good will of his supply sergeant, who undoubtedly would have borne the brunt of my disappointment and frustration with straight-faced indifference. By passively depending then, on an individual with no stake in my success, I gave him the option to defeat me, and he took that option.

I sat at my desk for more than an hour, my arms folded behind my neck, counting the holes in the asbestos ceiling tiles above me. I then decided to shift into an active mode (which I now do without staring at ceiling tiles for an hour); and did the following. I had the name of the major and the name of the sergeant, and their campus addresses. I wrote a gracious letter to the major, thanking him for his time, and acknowledging the fact that he had offered me a spotter-scope for my Cape Cod field work. I let him know how much I appreciated his help, and how useful the scope would be in my study. I apologized for not visiting his supply sergeant immediately to pick up the scope, as he had suggested, but I had to rush to a previous appointment. I wondered if he would be kind enough to call the sergeant and have the spotter-scope waiting for me that Friday afternoon, as I was leaving for Cape Cod that evening. And I asked him to note that I was sending a copy of this letter: (1) to his sergeant, to let him know that I will be picking up the spotter-scope on Friday; (2) to his boss, the army colonel who was in charge of the campus R.O.T.C. unit, to let him know that he has a good executive officer working for him; (3) to my own department chairman, who would be grateful for the cooperation I was receiving from the R.O.T.C. department; and (4) to the university provost, who, in the past, had gone on record as opposing an R.O.T.C. unit on his campus, but who would be happy to hear how that unit was helping a graduate student undertake his thesis field work. (In my later years I fine-tuned this technique. It's called "sand-bagging" an adversary, and it has several interesting options.) The letters went out in the campus mail on Tuesday. Friday afternoon, I stopped off at the supply sergeant's office. I found a spotter-scope boxed up and waiting for me. It was their newest model.

39 | LEAA LEVITY ON THE LEGAL ELEVATOR

Honing skills, III

You've got to believe me when I tell you that the last thing I wanted to do was to make any trouble. In fact I really don't even know what the outcome of my action was. And that's really the point—and the beauty of it.

I had been meeting at the Department of Justice with some justice lawyers. I was with EPA at the time and involved in a major environmental case dealing with the ecological damage incurred through the discharge of heated effluent from a Florida nuclear power plant into shallow coastal waters. We had taken a lunch break in the Department's cavernous basement cafeteria, and the whole lunchroom was filled with the most variegated agglomeration of human beings I had ever seen. You may not remember, but back then (we're talking about the early seventies, there was a federal organization (long-since disbanded) called the Law Enforcement Assistance Agency (LEAA). Part of the justice department, its purpose was to provide federal assistance to the nation's multitude of law enforcement agencies. (I've always thought that was a good idea, and have no clue as to why it was abandoned, or dis-created, as we say inside the Beltway. Most things I like get canceled, especially TV series, but that's another story.) Apparently there was a national LEAA conference being held upstairs, and the cafeteria was filled with every variety of sheriff, marshall, state trooper, county mountie, deputy, and just plain policeman. Uniforms of every type and color emblazoned the lunchroom, and the people wearing those uniforms were, to a person, grim- and serious-faced. There were more stern faces per cubic inch of space than you would find in a Shakespeare tragedy.

So then and there, I decided to do something innocently wicked. I didn't at first know exactly what it would be, and it didn't come to me until I found myself, with my two lawyer friends, in a rather huge elevator climbing from the basement cafeteria. Aside from the three of us, everyone else was a lawman, somber and straight. At least twenty of them, colorfully adorned and armed, numerically, with everything from .38 specials to .44 magnums, crowded the elevator. They were headed for an upper floor where their LEAA conference was being held. The three of us were getting off on the floor below, and as the door opened and my two lawyer friends stepped out, I knew what I had to do. I began walking out, patting my pocket and looking perplexed.

As the elevator door was closing, I spun around, faced the startled occupants, and pointing at them, I shouted, "Hey, one of these guys just lifted my wallet" I could only see the start of forty eyebrows raising and twenty mouths dropping as the door slid closed. I've often wondered what ensued inside that elevator during the next minute or two.

You could be what you should be, if you would be what you aren't

Think of the creative and imaginative abilities of the world population as occupying a huge normal bell curve. At the thinly populated back end of the curve are the true dull-ards, laggards, and those barely hanging on. They initiate nothing, contribute nothing, and are merely dragged along life's roadways; they are lackluster examples of apathetic existence at its worst. In the middle of the bell curve we find the vast majority of the population. It is a staggering continuum of characteristics and personalities, ranging from the very best to the not-so-good, from the notably creative to marginally sensitive. These folks are the basic receptors of ideas, fads, and fashion. Depending on which portion of the central curve they occupy, this population will either (1) eagerly accept a new idea, (2) cautiously phase in a suggested new way of doing things, (3) adopt a wait-and-see attitude before committing to any new concept, or (4) thoroughly resist even a hint of change.

Finally, at the front end of this statistical population, we find the world's tiny source of creative initiative: artists and writers, poets and politicians, scholars and scientists; thinkers and doers all. This small group of *individuals*—and I stress the word individuals—bears responsibility for defining the pathways and byways of the very life-roads we travel.

Granted, no matter what our own predilections and pref-erences, we are inexorably channeled into a particular life-road as a result of the random economic context and chance circumstances of our time and place of birth. Your birth— that event, at that moment, defines and marks your own start-point on a particular life-road. That is a given, and for most of the world's population, that start-point is but a hairline short of the ultimate end point. Most of us end up not much further along than where we started from. Why is this so? One big reason is that a presumption is categorically impressed upon the ego, by genetics or environment (or a combination of both) that declares it impossible or impractical for anyone to move outside or beyond his own "predestined" and "ordained" fate. This is hogwash.

It should be a cardinal goal for each of us to propel ourselves, to the fullest extent possible, along the positive axis of the bell curve I have just described. Again, the vast majority of us do not move at all. Some unfortunates find themselves, by dint of personal and/or professional catastrophe, inching along *backwards*. It is my belief, however, that one of humankind's more enduring (and endearing) characteristics, one that clearly separates us from our Darwinian cousins, is our capacity to reason, and our ability to motivate others to reason. It is this that carries us beyond the singular life-road chosen for us by the chance time and place of our birth.

I cannot define a specific formula to enhance your own creative and intuitive proclivities. Nonetheless, I can assure you that these talents will naturally increase within you as you turn your efforts toward amplifying your own confidence and self-esteem. The more confidence and self-esteem you possess, the more you will accomplish. The more you will accomplish, the more confidence and self-esteem you will possess. Remember that ram-jet? There is no better way to push yourself beyond your own original life-road, no better way to test and then to enhance your strength than *by working alone*. You will find yourself moving, bit by bit, along new and exciting paths, ever pointing yourself toward the creative end of that global bell curve. Some of you will get there. When you do, make certain to look me up. We'll have a lot to talk about!

41 THE NONDISCLOSURE STATEMENT

" . . . don't fence me in"

Every consulting agreement will include a nondisclosure statement (NDS). The NDS is constructed to protect both the consultant and the client. The client must know that whatever (1) materials he places at the disposal of the consultant, (2) discussions are undertaken with him, and (3) activities are pursued with him, these will not leave the client's physical and intellectual premises. For his part, the consultant is protected by the wording of the NDS from any frivolous claims made by an unsatisfied client. Further, the NDS will usually include a noncompetition clause (NCC) that references a following exhibit in which the consultant's tasks are spelled out. The NCC says something like

"The Consultant, now hired by Mighty Large Corporation, Inc. (MLCI), during the term of this Agreement, and for a period of 6 months thereafter, shall not provide the same or directly related services covered in Exhibit A, following, to any third party or parties, or for the Consultant's own account if the Consultant provides services or products that compete with MLCI."

This is one of several standard NDS/NCC formats that have been published elsewhere, and I will not replicate the various optional wordings here. However, there is a point that has to be made as to special language that *must* be incorporated into the standard NDS by consultants as myself, who, as part of their regular activities, present regular briefings on particular subjects to their whole stable of clients. I specifically present regular updates on the status and activities of government programs, budgets, and expectations. These updates have a core of standard information, to which I append specific materials of particular interest to that client, depending upon my perception of that client's needs. All of my presentations result in detailed and prolonged discussions with the client.

Invariably, the NDS I am asked to sign, before beginning work with a new client, will include a paragraph similar to the MLCI one cited above; thus preventing me from using my own knowledge to brief other private sector entities on topics similar to the ones I am being paid to brief that particular client. There is no need to get upset over this. This is standard NDS boilerplate language. However, though it may apply to several categories of "consultant," it certainly does not apply to my kind. And I always, and immediately, let the client know that I cannot be prevented from using my own knowledge to brief others—even his competitors. (I cannot, of course, use knowledge gained by my work for MLCI to brief another client. That would be a clear violation of principle and ethics.) I would explain to MLCI that I acquire data and information, and make my living by digesting and compressing these "brain-bits" and converting them to specific knowledge. Then I point out that I disseminate that knowledge, in the form of consultations, seminars, and lectures to companies such as his own. I also make two other points:

(1) If he wants to hire me *exclusively* for a period of time, then that is another matter, and we will negotiate a compensation fee commensurate with that activity, taking into account the income I would lose by refusing all other work for that period of time. (That has happened only once, and it resulted in a dizzyingly large-income, two-month contract with a west-coast aerospace company); and

(2) If he insists on retaining restrictive NDS language, while refusing to hire me at my outrageous "exclusive" rate, then I have no choice but to decline his offer of work. (That, too, has happened only once.)

What usually happens is that I am able to convince my new client that there are indeed several services, as listed in his Exhibit A of the NDS/NCC, that should be excluded from the restrictions imposed by that article of the contract agreement. And very clearly then, we insert, right into the same NDS, words such as

> "Services described in items 1, 3, 4, 5, and 8 of Paragraph A of Exhibit A are specifically excluded from the restriction of this article."

The best NDS I know is a short, simply stated document that is understandable and reflects the principle of common sense. The worst NDS I have seen went on for fourteen pages and would have required the interpretation by a staff of lawyers, had I signed it. Whatever NDS you do negotiate, make certain it contains a little sentence like the one above. Don't leave home without it.

42 | LIONS AND TIGERS AND BEARS

Group-gropes are only as good—or as bad—as the individual groper

A few weeks ago I was waiting in a Washington, D.C. hotel for a limo to take me to Dulles airport. I happened to look at the hotel's "Daily Event" sheet, and noticed a meeting that sounded interesting was taking place that very moment. It was being sponsored by an organization of local entrepreneurs, who were having their monthly get-together. It was worth investigating, and as I had a forty-five-minute wait for the next limo, I decided to poke my nose into the meeting room—more curious than anything else.

There were about sixty people, mostly men my own age, scattered around the room. That was the first thing I'd noticed. Nobody was sitting next to anyone else, as if they feared either contamination, recognition, or merely private discussion. I took up a position at the rear of the room, close to a stack of oat-bran muffins. The speaker, who had already completed his presentation, was at the dais responding to a question from the floor. The question must have been something like, " . . . How do I know when to quit my day job before wandering into the world of the entrepreneur?" Because the speaker's response was, " . . . and never, never, abandon the security of your present position until you have absolutely no doubts, and are assured as to the income you will derive as an entrepreneur." The answer seemed to more than satisfy the questioner, who left the floor mike with what seemed like a patina of relief coating his brow.

Well, I thought, so much for boldness. Obviously I was in the wrong room. These are not entrepreneurs. I had inadvertently wandered into a meeting of the Washington Wishy-Washy Society. At any rate, the meeting then seemed to have reached a break, because at that point everybody began moving toward the back of the room where coffee, donuts, and I were planted. I turned to leave the room, oat-bran muffin in hand, and was stopped by a tap on the shoulder from the gentleman who had just been on stage. He introduced himself as the group's president, and said that he'd noticed my late entrance, and would I be interested in learning more about his organization. I looked at the clock on the wall, noted that I had another thirty minutes to wait for the limo, and feeling guilty about holding a purloined, half-eaten oat-bran muffin, I told him that I indeed would be interested. I will spare you the details. Suffice it say that his was a band of frightened pussycats peering around the corner together to make sure the neighborhood dog was still chained in his yard.

I learned that, under the rubric of a support group, the same sixty or so individuals meet on a regular basis to sigh together. They enwrap each other with the unfortunate circumstances surrounding their current employment and defame their supervisors. Then they plot and plan for the day when they will move out on their own as real entrepreneurs, and with pension in hand. They provide each other with viewgraphs, charts, and various handouts. And they plan and they plot. As this was being related to me, I rolled my eyeballs in mock sympathy and wrung my hands in mock agony. (Cheez! . . . I thought. All this bull for a not-so-great oat-bran muffin.) Finally, as the clock moved toward limo time, I asked the gentleman how many of the group, beside himself, had escaped the "high-security" prison (pun intended) of the salaried employee and had climbed Mount Entrepreneur. He responded that I had misunderstood. His was a support group for people who *want* to do it, but hadn't yet. He himself was still a twenty five-year manager at the Department of Education. Speechless, I simply stood up and found my way to the

limo—which turned out to be an airport taxi. The driver
was close to my own age. He spoke little (if any) English
and drove like a madman. But he understood more about
entrepreneurship than any of the fakes I had just left. He
handed me my luggage at the airport, and I knew I had
left him too large a tip. But it felt somehow appropriate
to do so.

43 | WRITE! RIGHT?

" . . . yes, I remember it well"

No, I really *don't* remember it well. Have you ever had your mind go blank just as you are introducing someone, a person you've known for thirty years? I have. It's really embarrassing. I never forget a name or a face. Anyone who knows me will confirm that. They will also confirm, after a moment or two, that I am often incapable of putting the correct name with the correct face! Such is one flaw of many I may admit to, but never in print (. . . oops).

The ability to recall names, dates, people, things, events, conversations, etc. will hold you, as a person working alone, in great stead. You have no one at the next desk to turn to and ask even the simplest question, which means that you must depend upon yourself to remember. If you are indeed blessed with total recall, then skip this essay entirely. Know first, however, that I envy you with all my might. . . . What did you say your name was?

As for me, the upper joint of the middle finger on my right hand is at least fifteen percent thicker than the corresponding joint on my left hand—that's where a pen or pencil presses—because I am forever writing things down. Whenever I go to a meeting or to a conference, be it formal or informal, or even a chance business encounter, I take notes. I have a small pad I always keep with me, and I always *write it down*.

This is not a real easy thing to do. At first it might even seem to be quite a chore. But it turns out to be a very smart thing to do, and it gets easier. Your notes may turn out to be the best, and many times the *only*, record of a meeting. You always end up rereading your notes, reviewing and refreshing your mind as to the points that were made and the actions that were to be taken. By not relying upon memory alone, you are creating a significant advantage for yourself.

Look around you the next time you are attending a business meeting, large or small. How many of the participants are taking notes? Probably the majority, the overwhelming majority, are not. Time and again I have been contacted after a meeting, and asked to certify whether so-and-so said this, or whether this-and-that was decided. Soon, you are considered the final arbiter as to the events that have unfolded at a meeting—from an actual action item to an *obiter dictum*.

Always remember, that to a great extent your income is proportionately related to your knowledge. And your knowledge is no greater than the sum of your memory. My own memory needs the help of the written word, and if yours does too, don't be lazy or ashamed or embarrassed. Whip out paper and pen. And use a Mont Blanc fountain pen, if you can. Mine always impresses the clients.

44 | FORCE MULTIPLIER

Do it once, use it often

The term "force multiplier" had its origins years ago among the word makers of our own Department of Defense. We had then expected the "asian horde" and the "evil empire" to muster tens of millions of troops, which would then be thrown against the meager, thin armies of the U.S./NATO/SEATO forces. It was necessary, then, to develop a strategy that would allow a numerically inferior allied troop structure to overwhelm a numerically superior opponent. The idea was to create a situation whereby a single soldier, well-trained and equipped, would be able to deliver sufficient firepower to defeat a force x times as large, where x would be a multiplier based on U.S. technological prowess. The result, a fully unleashed, technologically superior force, could then count on its better training and equipment to overpower a numerically superior enemy;—a result clearly seen in Desert Storm, where several hundred aircraft and their supporting forces (if left to complete their job) could have eliminated completely the entire Iraqi armed forces numbering several hundred thousand.

What has all this to do with working alone? Well, in a manner of speaking, everything! When you are working alone you must make every minute—or as many as possible—count. Others, bureaucrats, managers, professors, can get their forty-hour paychecks regularly, despite the fact that they may not work eight hours in an eight-hour day. However, if you are working alone, your income becomes related directly to your output. A two-and-a-half hour coffee break, during which time you contemplate your navel, may be an occasional recreational necessity. But if it becomes a self-stipulated daily requirement, rest assured you will soon be looking for a "regular" job.

More important, you have just so many hours in a day in which to create money. And this brings us to the concept of force multiplier. You can maximize your money-making efforts if you are able to do *one* thing and get paid for it several times. That becomes the ultimate key to self-reliance, satisfaction, and financial success for the person working alone.

I pursue the force multiplier concept as follows: You have noted, in pages past, that I've interspersed comments on both my newsletter and consulting activities. It is no accident that these two enterprises occupy my time. I have earlier called these, "symbiotic" activities. What I meant by that should now be clear. I do keep my newsletter and consulting functions physically separate, mainly for tax purposes. My office in the National Press Building is maintained for activities directly related to publishing my newsletters, and there I do no consulting. I carry on my consulting business out of a post-office box, and there I publish no newsletters (the P.O. box is too small to fit my fax—oh, that was terrible, sorry). Actually, my consulting office is in suburban Washington, D.C. (it's in my home—more about that elsewhere).

Both newsletter publishing and consulting, then, are physically separated, but, nonetheless, mentally joined. My consulting business grows by name recognition propagated through my newsletters. The newsletter subscription base increases by virtue of my clients' desire to keep up with events related to their businesses. And superimposed over these two is a third, ever-growing business, that of public speaking. As one's name and reputation spread through an ever-growing newsletter and consulting effort, so do requests by organizations eager to listen to you first-hand at luncheons, seminars, and short-courses. And the amazing truth is that often—in fact, *most* of the time—a single effort,

126 Murray Felsher, Ph.D.

only slightly altered, can be "sold" to satisfy the requirements of a newsletter article, a client's request, and a speaking engagement.

To illustrate this last point by example:

I was asked by a magazine to submit an article addressing instances of environmental remote sensing from space. Specifically, it was to deal with actual examples of monitoring and assessing environmental degradation using instruments aboard existing earth-orbiting satellites. No problem. That's my field. It took me a good two weeks to gather my notes (of course, I was doing other things as well) and prepare the article. In the twelve-months following submission of that article I used the very same materials to

(1) prepare a "white paper" for distribution at a Congressional Hearing,
(2) write four articles in my *Washington Remote Sensing Letter*,
(3) write one article in my *Washington Federal Science Newsletter*,
(4) brief three industrial clients,
(5) brief one federal agency client,
(6) brief one state agency client,
(7) make presentations at two national meetings.

This is a classic example—a definitive example—of employing the force multiplier concept. It is so much easier, and more gratifying, to concentrate on doing a job if you know that you are, at the same time, laying the groundwork for additional income down the road. The trick is to always keep the client/subscriber/audience happy by providing each exactly what he wants for his money. You will find that your own eight-hour day will ultimately produce dozens of days of income. May the "force" be with you!

45 | TO WORK, PERHAPS TO LOAF

Maybe you *should* keep the day job

As a federal employee, I once conducted an informal experiment with my colleagues. It went as follows: I asked several of my federal friends to track *every minute* of a single typical day at work. I asked them to log, minute-by-minute, their entire workday, just to see for themselves how they really were spending their time. One refused. In retrospect, I believe he knew what the result would show, and he wanted no part of it. I participated as well, and on the designated day (the same for all of us), we logged "A Day in the Working Life of a Bureaucrat." The results were indeed fascinating. Though the eight of us, (seven, plus me), all mid-level managers, were in four different agencies, the results were remarkably similar. For an eight-hour day, they averaged out to

(1) Coming into the office and "settling in"	10 minutes
(2) Talking with subordinates, not work-related	25 minutes
(3) Talking with peers, not work-related	40 minutes
(4) Talking with supervisors, not work-related	10 minutes
(5) Talking on the telephone, not work-related	15 minutes
(6) Reading a newspaper, not work-related	15 minutes

(7) Sitting at the desk, not work-related, (other)	20 minutes
(8) Stretching one's legs, walking the halls	20 minutes
(9) Official coffee breaks	30 minutes
(10) Bathroom	30 minutes
(11) Water fountain	15 minutes
(12) Closing up "shop" for the day	25 minutes
Total	255 minutes

The total amount of time thus spent *not* working in an average 8-hour day was 41/4 hours. A good 53.2 percent of our time was spent *not* doing what we were being paid to do.

Mind you, I am convinced that these numbers are not spurious. The reason is that, being thoroughly intrigued by my little federal experiment, I then expanded it to include industry and academe. I called mid- to high-level management friends in the private sector. Then I called several classmates who had received their Ph.D.s when I did, but unlike me had remained as professors in universities. They all undertook the same one-day experiment for me. Their answers, though statistically unfit even for the *Journal of Irreproducible Results*, do bear some consideration. From our earlier experiment, we knew that federal bureaucrats worked 3 hours and 45 minutes. We discovered that their counterparts in industry averaged 5 hours and 35 minutes, and my professor friends averaged 3 hours and thirty minutes. Try that little experiment for yourself, and you will begin to see why the "work ethic" in the United States may be no more than a "myth ethic," and why we are losing the race in international competitiveness.

There are some basic choices to be made here. The up-side of working alone is that you get to keep what you make—and you could make a lot. It's a very self-centered way to live, granted. And you must possess, or be willing to learn *how* to possess, a mind-set geared to a true work ethic. Further, you're working for yourself, and you're not really involved with anyone else's problems; but then, no one is involved with your problems either. You must be self-reliant and truly enjoy doing what you are doing. But if you are the kind of person who chooses to dally away hour after hour, day after day, happy to collect your salary and adhere to the time tabulations above, then please, for your own sake, stay where you are. And I promise not to tell anyone that you are reading this book.

46 | IT'S NOT *WHO* YOU KNOW, IT'S WHO PEOPLE *THINK* YOU KNOW, THAT COUNTS

Honing skills, IV

No, I don't know J. W. Marriott, nor his son, nor his son's sons. I stay at his hotels, but I don't know his family. The closest I ever came to them was a decade or so ago, when our own number-one son, now completing his doctorate in nuclear engineering, was awarded his Eagle Scout badge. The Marriotts sponsored a major ceremony at the Kennedy Center for all new Washington-area Eagle Scouts, and we attended. The Marriotts were little dots on the Kennedy Center concert stage—that's as close as I ever got to them.

Nevertheless, I do enjoy their hotels. I recently found myself exiting an airport limo at the entrance to a newly built Marriott in San Antonio, Texas. Stepping out of the limo, I asked the driver why there were three men scrubbing down the (seemingly spotless) exterior ground tiles at the hotel entrance. He explained to me that the hotel was expecting a visit the next day from several Marriotts themselves, who were descending on Texas turf to inspect this new facility.

I walked into a rather crowded lobby, and made my way to the registration desk. The clerk was polite and cheerful, but had to inform me that it would be another half-hour or so until my room would be ready. In all fairness, I must say that it was only 10:00 A.M., and the hotel was full up with two major conventions. Still, I did have a luncheon appointment at Riverwalk, and I wanted to peel off the travel grime. So I did what comes naturally, that is, to ask the clerk, without preface, what time the Marriotts were expected tomorrow. Startled, she punched up my reservation again, while asking me how I knew they were being visited by members of the ruling family. By now, she had my reservation information on her computer screen, including my suburban Maryland address. I must now tell you that Marriott world headquarters is also in suburban Maryland, Bethesda, to be exact. I responded that the Marriotts are Maryland neighbors. Not a lie. Not even a fib. We occupy space in the same state. Their headquarters and my offices are within fifteen miles of each other! Of course, I didn't say that to the clerk. I merely said that the Marriotts are Maryland neighbors.

Well, maybe she thought that I was an advance man for the Marriott party. I mean, I did nothing to dissuade her, or *per*suade her. I just smiled. She upgraded my unavailable king-sized, nonsmoking room to a suddenly available upper-floor corner suite overlooking Riverwalk on the concierge level, no extra charge. She hoped I would enjoy my stay. She didn't know, but I was already enjoying my stay.

47 PUBLIC SPEAKING

I think, therefore I am, but I speak, therefore I get paid . . . sometimes

It is always to your benefit and advantage to be well known. The more people who know you and what you do, the larger the universe of potential clients, subscribers, customers, attendees, participants, patrons, and purchasers you have. The old saw, the one that says something like, " . . . write anything you want about me or my business, but make sure you spell the names right," is right on the button. One of the easiest ways to enlarge that universe is to immerse oneself, to the extent plausible, into the public-speaking arena. The very good thing about presenting a talk to a group is that, by definition, it is an activity that is expected to be undertaken alone. Oh sure, in a technical society meeting, a professional paper is often authored by several individuals. Yet, even there, it is but a lone individual at the dais making the presentation for the group. And by the way, if you *do* find yourself as a coauthor of a technical paper, make certain that *you* are the one making the actual presentation, even if you are not listed as the first, or senior, author.

Within the realm of public speaking, I would have you consider three categories: (1) A freebie. You receive no monetary compensation. (2) You are paid expenses only. (3) You are paid a fee plus expenses.

The types and varieties of each are endless, and examples of each follow:

(1) Freebies. You receive no monetary compensation.

  A. *Professional Society Activities*
1. You present a poster session
2. You present a technical paper
3. You are a member of a technical committee
4. You are chairman of a technical committee
5. You are chairman of a technical session
6. You are an invited panelist
7. You are an invited speaker
8. You are a technical program chairman
9. You are an invited luncheon speaker
10. You are an invited dinner speaker
11. You are an invited plenary keynote speaker

  B. *Educational Activities*
1. You are asked to speak to elementary school students
2. You are asked to deliver a lecture at a local high school

  C. *Executive Branch Activities, in Washington, D.C.*
1. You make an initial briefing to a government agency staff

  D. *Legislative Branch Activities in Washington, D.C.*
1. You are invited to brief a congressional staff
2. You are invited to brief a congressional caucus
3. You are invited to testify at a congressional hearing

  E. *Media Activities*
1. You provide a sound bite on a radio/TV newscast
2. You are interviewed on radio/TV

  F. *Public Interest Activities*
1. You serve on local civic committees

And we could go on and on. The common thread among all of the examples above, is that no money at all ever changes hands. You undertake all—and indeed I have—at no charge (if not *pro bono publico*, then at least *a plaisir*). For whatever is your own ultimate rationale for having so given of your precious time, and it can run the gamut from

ego to guilt, one of the reasons *must* be to splash your
name across the landscape. You must let people know of
your existence and the availability of the product/service
you are offering. This is not a selfish or a cynical motive; it
is merely a basic fact of life. If no one knows you, then you
might as well stay in bed and pull the sheet over your head.
When you are working alone, it is indeed the squeaking
wheel that gets the oil. And there is no better way to get
the attention of the fellow with the oilcan than to undertake
an active public-speaking stance, even if it entails a lot of
freebies as in (1) above. Please also note, however, that
there are *no* examples in (1) (and by jiminy there never
will be an example) of *my* work for a private sector entity
with no remuneration. Now to the next:

(2) You are paid expenses only. These are some examples
of public-speaking that paid my out-of-pocket expenses,
but no fee:
   A. *As an invited speaker at*
      1. any service organization or lodge
      2. any business group
      3. any graduate business school
      4. most public colleges or universities
      5. some private colleges and universities
   B. *As an invited member of*
      1. any federal agency advisory panel
      2. any board of advisors to a professional meeting
      3. any local or state government task force
      4. any privately sponsored panel advising the gov-
         ernment
      5. any international workshop or meeting

These examples will (should) always offer to pay your
out-of-pocket expenses. If an offer is not made to pay
expenses, and I expect to be reimbursed for these outlays,
I immediately say something like, " . . . and I am assuming
that you will defray my expenses." If they say no, then I
say no. Sometimes I decline the offer of paid expenses and
pay out of my own pocket. If, for instance, I am giving a

talk at a not-so-wealthy public university, within a short distance of where I happen to have other business, I will decline the offer to cover expenses. In instances where air travel and hotel expenses are involved I usually accept the offer. Private colleges and universities usually will fall into category (3), below. The only hard rule I have is to charge the federal government either my expenses or my expenses plus fee. I always take the government's money. It is not wise to get a federal bureaucrat used to the idea that he can use your brain and not pay for it. He usually ends up trying to make a habit of it. Always take what Uncle Sam offers, ask when he doesn't offer, demand when he refuses to offer, and threaten to inform the agency Inspector General (IG) if he doesn't pay when he should have. (Federal bureaucrats live in mortal fear of very few things. Two of these things are [1] his agency's IG and [2] the U.S. Congress' General Accounting Office [GAO]. I have seen the most arrogant, pretentious, and autocratic martinets wither into jelly when informed they are being investigated by auditors from either the IG or GAO.)

Category (3) is where the money is. Here are several examples of public speaking where I have received a significant fee, over and above reimbursement for actual expenses incurred:

(3) You are paid a fee plus expenses.
  1. Lecturing or presenting a seminar at a private college or university
  2. Teaching a full course as a visiting professor at any college or university
  3. Organizing and presenting my own short course to my technical peers
  4. Organizing and presenting my own seminar or workshop to the public.

The first two examples are relatively low-return, effortless activities. The last two can quickly become major time-consuming efforts, albeit significant cash-cows.

My point, then, is that you must strike your own balance

as to exactly how much public speaking you can afford
to undertake. Your decision should be based on only two
variables: (A) your time and (B) your ego. Whatever else,
don't let (B) overcome (A), or you'll be overcommitted
when the *real* jobs start coming in. And remember, money
in must always exceed money *out*. Not so?

48 AUTHORSHIP

When I do, I don't write; when I write, I don't do

This book is being written in real time. By that I mean I am not disappearing into a locked room, with someone shoveling in food every few hours. And I am not going to emerge into sunlight after a couple of weeks with a manuscript tucked under my arm. No. I must still write three newsletters every two weeks. I must collect data, contact people, and continually take care of a thousand items. I still have obligations to my consulting clients, and I must still maintain all my usual contacts, as well as make new ones. This means that I write this book when I can. And when I can't, I don't. But hey, that's what working alone is all about! I'm certain that this manuscript will indeed be pressed between covers, and the words I am now writing will reside (for not too long) on shelves in bookstores throughout the country. I started writing this four months ago, and I expect, if I continue at the same rate, to be finished three months hence. The writing is being done in a somewhat random fashion. The individual topics, as they appear in this book, impress themselves on my mind, one at a time, and I note them down. When I find I have an hour or two, I take out my notes and sit down at the computer, or take out my pad and pen on an airplane (I haven't yet found a Macintosh portable I like) and begin composing.

I don't have in front of me exactly what it was I wrote last week or last month, and sometimes I wonder whether, as

I write today, I am contradicting something I have already written. I also wonder how much I'm leaving out, and will I remember to include thoughts that seemed so important when I awoke suddenly at 3:00 A.M. this morning, most of which I immediately forgot. I also wonder, if I sit down by the fireplace and read the whole manuscript from page one, will I still respect me in the morning?

49 | ROUGHING-UP THE DOLLAR

Don't round-up and don't round-down

When submitting a proposal to a client you may be tempted to round-up the bottom-line dollar request to the nearest higher good-looking number, with lots of zeros. There may be an occasion when you feel it is necessary to provide this primal padding. (In fact, I recall telling you earlier of an instance when I did that very thing.) But it should be done rarely, and with certain care. The last thing you want to do is to have the community pass the word that you are always "rounding-up" to the nearest thousand or ten thousand, and thereby have your clients automatically reduce all your proposals by x percent. No, do it rarely. And if "rarely" turns out to be "never," then all the better. (Of course you will *never* "round-*down*" your cost estimates—but you already know that.) However, please consider "roughing-up", not "rounding-up" your numbers, to wit:

Whether you are submitting a proposal to a private sector or government client, the recipient of your proposal will be a person of the "bean-counter" persuasion—a number cruncher. His perception of your proposal, will often (if not usually) commence as he bypasses your technical pages and turns to your "cost" section, noting the dollar amount you are requesting. His impression can be positively influenced by a simple technique. That technique is your marked attention to detail as reflected by "roughing-up" the amount of money you are asking. If you want $10,000, ask for

$10,165. If you want $350,000, ask for $353,981. Like that. Get it? A proposal constructed to conclude with an odd-dollar request is automatically (in alphabetical order), accurate, compelling, convincing, correct, legitimate, solid, and valid. You stickler for detail, you.

To speak out, perhaps to *freak* out—there's the rub

"It's better to keep your mouth shut and be assumed a fool than to open it and remove all doubt," saith Twain. "When in doubt, mumble," saith Boren. "No one ever got into trouble because of something he *didn't* say," saith I-don't-know-who. There are dozens of clever ways to confirm that trouble comes to most people when they say something they shouldn't.

Many people are burdened by a compulsion that requires them to comment on everything. This self-directed activity is particularly devastating in the workplace environment, where such comments are often the basis for career advancement, stagnation, or termination. A salaried employee has the ability, should he be clever enough to cultivate it, of keeping his mouth closed and his options open. He will still find himself collecting his paycheck at the end of the week. The consultant working alone, however, does not have that luxury. As a consultant you have been contracted to transfer your knowledge to the client. That transfer takes place in the form of communication, both written and oral.

You may sometimes find yourself in a position where you are asked to respond to a question by the person paying your invoice—and you don't feel it appropriate to answer that question. The question may be (1) of a personal nature or (2) too argumentative.

A full and honest response may (1) require you to divulge information of a confidential nature, (2) disclose sensitive

141

sources, (3) result in a direct conflict of interest, or (4) place you at a competitive disadvantage.

For whatever other reasons you come up with, you may simply think the question is unacceptable, and any answer you may give would be inappropriate.

This is a sticky situation. On one hand, it does not do you any good to be indignant and thus create an adversarial situation,—especially if the questioner is of the short-fuse type. On the other hand, if you respond fully, you leave yourself open to other difficulties,—especially with this client, who would now feel he has you "in his pocket," and can then press for additional information on the basis of intellectual blackmail. As I say, it's a difficult situation. Like most difficult situations though, there is an easy way out. Simply, it is to never let yourself get *into* the situation in the first place.

You know whether you are being confronted with such a situation if you feel that you should mentally zip your mouth to prevent any outflow of substantial numbers of words, lest by their bulk those very same words will be used to bury you. And physically you want to do very little more than shake your head and mumble, "no," or nod your head and mumble, "yes." So what do you do? This is what you do. As soon as you are asked to provide a verbal or written statement that you believe is not appropriate, you must refuse to do so. Period. To refuse at the outset is relatively easy, as opposed to a later refusal which may become impossible. The more you respond, the more you are expected to respond. Eventually word will get out and your reputation will evaporate, together with your business.

To the epigrams at the head of this piece, allow me to add the following ten-word phrase that I would have you commit to memory. It goes, " . . . I'm sorry, but that's outside the scope of our agreement," saith Felsher. Memorize it. Use it.

51 OBLIGATIONS

It sometimes rains, but it always stops

"... It's not easy being me.
     Master of me own destiny,
     Admiral of me own ship at sea ..."

So sings The Commodore, Robin Williams' "pappy," in that wonderfully bizarre movie version of "Popeye." Movie criticism aside (I still think it was one of the finest Hollywood products of the decade), the message is one you must take to heart. The up-side of working alone is the shedding of responsibilities to bosses, managers, supervisors, and that whole universe of chain of command. Yes, you have "unchained" yourself from the onus of external reporting requirements. But you have substituted in its stead a far more stringent and severe set of *internal* requirements. You can no longer praise, depend upon, credit, or blame subordinates or supervisors for your own actions and results. More important, you have in a very real sense, only *you* standing between your family's well-being and financial doom. This is a serious matter, not to be taken lightly, and always to be considered.

You have significant and ever-present obligations to your loved ones that must continually be met by you and you alone. The pressure that accompanies this omnipresent realization may become too great. I have known several good men who were unable to continue working on their own and have returned to the salaried life, solely as a result of the high level of sustained pressure they placed upon themselves to always

143

succeed. Even the slightest and most temporary setback can evoke a sense of panic in such individuals. The result can easily be the initiation of a slide away from entrepreneurial commitment back into the comfortable world of corporate oblivion. I urge you to give yourself every chance to succeed. Do not relish the occasional failure, but be at ease with it.

A backwards step does not, in itself, define a trend. And just so, remember that "trend" is not "destiny." The direction in which you move and the pattern it establishes is a function of your own pointing mechanisms. In the end, you must balance your own understanding of occasional setbacks with your own expectations of ultimate success. This does not come easy, but it is a lesson that must be learned by any "admiral of his own ship . . ." If you do it right, you *will* prevail. As The Commodore says in the same song; " . . . I'm strong to the finish, 'cause I eats me spinach . . ."

Stay the course. Eat your spinach. Take care of your family.

There is a time for boldness and there is a time for caution

I'm sitting at the writing desk in my room at the Newton, Massachusetts, Marriott. There is a large picture window beside me, overlooking an arm of the Charles River. The river is partially frozen over, and flocks of Canadian geese are parked on the ice's edge,—doing whatever parked geese do. As I watch, a vee of a dozen or so geese comes flying into view. Instead of selecting an azimuth for a straight-in direct landing, they bank right, into a stiff, icy wind, beat their wings, bank right, again, coast a bit, lose some altitude, and continue their slow, cautious, spiral descent. They make three wide circles, and finally, their leader, seemingly satisfied, presses his legs forward, lets the air fall out of his wings, and settles down on the ice edge.

I'm going to let you in on my little secret about what to do with some of the money you are going to make working alone. You're going to put it into the stock market. Yes, I know, you didn't purchase this book to read about the stock market. Goodness knows there are hundreds of thousands of words written and spoken daily on that most devious of subjects; words by experts who, if they really knew what they were writing and talking about, would be very rich. But alas, the stock market is the very worst possible crapshoot. Its ups and downs follow no predestined, predetermined, or predictable pattern; and if you are a person of the gambling persuasion I strongly recommend that you buy a ticket to

Atlantic City or Las Vegas—the odds are much better there than they are on Wall Street.

In order to succeed on Wall Street you have to be a cautious goose, landing ever so slowly and gently on that cold, wet ice. The key to success is to eschew the "big play." Bank on the single,—the *only*, certainty to prevail in the financial canyons of lower Manhattan. That certainty is, with Newtonian regularity, *Whatever Goes Up Must Come Down* and, inversely Newtonian, *Whatever Comes Down Must Go Up*. A good friend, whose business card says he is a financial advisor, once confided in me the secret of success. "Buy low," he said, "and sell high." I take him at his word.

Let me tell you what I do. I selected *one*, publicly traded company, and learned all I possibly could about that company. I mean *all*. That means it had to be a small company, preferably without a substantial corporate history, and preferably close to its initial public offering. This means that the company stock, being immature and unable to sustain a price range on its own merits, will ride the coattails of the market as a whole. The market can be counted on to provide a material buffer for that stock, and it will rise and fall in comfortable and gentle, if not predictable, cycles. I buy and sell that one company's stock. Only that stock and no other. I have abandoned stockbrokers who have urged me, with words of avarice and greed, to plunge into other stocks, like a goose into icy waters. Since its first offering, my stock has moved between 11 and 23, and I move with it. I always buy it whenever it is below 14 and I always sell it whenever it is above 20. I never buy it when it is above 20 and I never sell it when it is below 14. In between 14 and 20 I buy or sell, depending on which way the market as a whole is moving. These numbers are, of course, subject to change as the stock's high and low points change. You don't make much all at once, but you don't lose much all at once either. What you end up doing is making a little, most of the time. But it does add up. This began for me as an intellectual hobby; it is now a serious business. But not *that* serious. I still make slow, careful circles, and I'm still very careful where exactly I'm settling my fanny down.

53 | WASHINGTON FEDERAL SCIENCE NEWSLETTER

Newsletters, III

Why not, I thought. *Washington Remote Sensing Letter* was churning along nicely. ATC was keeping me busy. But I found I still I had a little time and a lot of energy left over at the end of the day. So why not start a second newsletter? After all, I was now an official editor and publisher—subscribers, credentials, and National Press Building office all vouched for that. The more I thought about it, the more I liked the idea. My expenses would increase, but not double. My office rent, utilities, and related expenses would remain the same whether I published one newsletter or two. Printing and postage costs would go up, of course, but if I structured the second newsletter along the same lines as the first, it would be profitable. So that's what I did.

The thing I first did was to look around for a newsletter idea that was not already taken. I am told that there are more than 20,000 newsletters published in the U.S. of A., and I expected it would be somewhat difficult to discover a subject that wasn't already saturated. I knew the *WRSL* idea was unique (and still is—there is no other privately owned, subscriber-supported, regularly published, globally distributed newsletter dealing solely with satellite remote sensing of the earth. There wasn't in 1981 and there isn't now). In a way that made it easy. It's always fun (not to mention profitable) filling an open, but hitherto unrecognized niche. But this was different. What I needed was a subject matter that I (1) found interesting, (2) knew something about, one that had (3) a readily available information base, and (4) an inexpensive or free information source.

I looked around, and there, all about me, was the answer. The richest source of information, worldwide, is the U.S. federal establishment. Hundreds of thousands of federal employees around the country are paid trillions of dollars in salaries to create warehouses of data on every conceivable subject. These data bundles are funneled into agency and department headquarters' offices here in Washington, D.C., where tens of thousands of workers squeeze, massage, and otherwise manipulate the data to create information packages that will make them and their supervisors look good. And, finally, to inform the public of all the good they are doing, the Washington, D.C. federal establishment has hired hundreds of the very best editors, writers, and public affairs specialists whose single role in life is to crank out news releases as fast as their copying machines can produce them. It's all there, and it's all free.

I decided that my second newsletter would be devoted to reporting science and technology activities of the federal government. I sat down and listed, off the top of my head, those agencies which contained a science or engineering component I could count on to produce reportable items on a regular basis. These are the actual (alphabetized) first pages of that initial scratch-sheet list:

Executive Branch
   A. *Office of the President*
      (1) Council on Environmental Quality
      (2) Economic Policy Council
      (3) National Space Council
      (4) Office of Management and Budget
      (5) Office of National Drug Control Policy
      (6) Office of Regulatory Affairs and Information
      (7) Office of Science and Technology Policy
   B. *Agriculture Department*
      (1) Agricultural Cooperative Service
      (2) Agricultural Marketing Service
      (3) Agricultural Research Service

(4) Agricultural Stabilization and Conservation Service
(5) Animal and Plant Health Inspection Service
(6) Commodity Programs and International Affairs
(7) Cooperative State Research Service
(8) Economic Research Service
(9) Extension Service
(10) Federal Grain Inspection Service
(11) Food and Nutrition Service
(12) Food Safety and Inspection Service
(13) Foreign Agricultural Service
(14) Forest Service
(15) Human Nutrition Information Service
(16) National Agricultural Library
(17) National Agricultural Statistics Service
(18) Office of the Consumer Advisor
(19) Office of Energy
(20) Rural Electrification Administration
(21) Soil Conservation Service

C. *Commerce Department*
(1) Bureau of the Census
(2) Bureau of Economic Analysis
(3) Bureau of Export Administration
(4) Economic Development Administration
(5) International Trade Administration
(6) National Institute of Standards and Technology (was National Bureau of Standards)
(7) National Oceanic and Atmospheric Administration
(8) National Technical Information Service
(9) National Telecommunications and Information Adm.
(10) Patent and Trademark Office

Now, I'm not going to detail that complete first list; to do so would require too many pages. Suffice it to say that it covered the technical units within the remaining twelve departments (Defense, Education, Energy, Health and Human Services, Housing and Urban Development,

Interior, Justice, Labor, State, Transportation, Treasury, and the new Department of Veteran Affairs). It also covered those of the seventy-three independent federal agencies with technical components. Some of these are well-known; such as Environmental Protection Agency, National Aeronautics and Space Administration, Nuclear Regulatory Commission, and National Science Foundation. Others are not household names; such as Office of the Nuclear Waste Negotiator, Federal Mine Safety and Health Review Commission, Consumer Product Safety Commission, and Federal Maritime Commission. In addition, I listed those units of the legislative branch I could count on to provide me with information. Among those are Congressional Research Service, Office of Technology Assessment, and General Accounting Office, plus the various house and senate science and technical committees.

In all, I was certain that I would not lack for information. And what was really great was that *all* of these offices provided fully written, technically accurate press releases, free of charge. All I had to do was to put my name on their mailing lists, which I did. My name, as it turns out, was "Publisher, *Washington Federal Science Newsletter*." I chose the word, "Newsletter" instead of "Letter," as I had done with *WRSL*, because I fully intended *WFSN* to be a straightforward reporting document, with no personal analysis or commentary—as opposed to *WRSL*, which was about 60 percent news and 40 percent opinion. I feel very comfortable offering my own identified biases to my *WRSL* readership, since I feel qualified, by professional background and experience in matters related to satellite remote sensing of the earth. However, if I am reproducing a science note from the Office of Nuclear Material Safety and Safeguards of the Nuclear Regulatory Commission, covering a subject I know nothing about, I would be loathe to offer any commentary at all. I would simply reproduce their press release.

Which brings me to a very important point. The press releases provided to the media by the federal establishment are *not copyrighted*. That means they can indeed be read, as is, on any television newscast or radio broadcast. Further, they can be reproduced, as is, in any newspaper or any newsletter. As it turns out, I digitally scan each release and import it to my word processor for minor editing. The main problem, as you would expect, is information-culling. I limit each issue to eight pages. *WFSN* subscription rates and frequency of publication are $310 to North America subscribers, and $400 to overseas subscribers; two times per month, except once per month in January and in August—22 times per year. At this point we . . . (even working alone, I sometimes use "we" when referring to the newsletters. Mark Twain said that the second-person reference is allowed if one is an editor, king, or suffering from tapeworm) . . . we, I say, are into our fifth year of publishing *WFSN*. And every now and then I find that an article I've prepared for *WFSN* is also applicable to the next issue of *WRSL*, and vice versa. There I am, muxing to the max. And wouldn't you know it, there still is not yet a newsletter comparable to *WFSN* on the street. The really breathtaking outlook is that, unlike *WRSL,* which has a total global subscriber potential of 40,000 to 50,000, the broad scientific and engineering coverage provided by *WFSN* opens its potential subscriber universe to numbers in the millions. WOW!

54 | WORKING AT HOME

Leaving the nest

Most people working alone start by working at home. Whether it be a consulting business, a newsletter business, a speaker's bureau, or any of the other solo activities pursued, it is natural to start within the confines, security, and comfort of one's own four walls. Depending on the actual nature of the business and the actual makeup of one's family, there are good reasons to work at home forever, or to get an outside office as fast as possible—and everything in between. My own "everything in between" came down to renting office space for my newsletter business and working at home for my consulting business.

Although I strongly believe in working alone, I do not believe in living alone. I have been blessed with a loving wife, who, for more than thirty years, has supported my strange decisions and the directions those decisions have taken us. I've always felt uncomfortable working for someone else, and so spent as many years as possible in schools around the country. I figured that the more years I spent at school, the fewer years I'd have to work—talk about strange! Thus, as a long-time "professional student," our family has lived in college towns in Massachusetts, Texas, California, and New York, not to mention a couple of towns in Ontario, Canada. Through all this, as well as the "real" (salaried) jobs I've had as a professor, educational administrator, and a federal technocrat, my wife has stood at my side. And I don't mean dormantly at my side. When

152

our oldest child passed her fourteenth birthday, my wife decided to go back to school for her master's degree. She then kept right on going and earned her Ph.D.

I guess we really supported each other's growth and achievements. This, I feel is the one most important reality that faces an individual who is considering a solo work-life; a single man or woman is indeed faced with other realities. A married person must have the total support of his or her spouse before even contemplating the precarious and unpredictable life that faces one working alone. In any case, once such a decision is made, be prepared for a whole set of changes; the initial, and perhaps most important, changes will be those that relate to working at home.

There are whole books devoted to "do's and don't's" in maintaining a home office. They deal with all aspects of working at home, ranging from office supply requirements to tax hints. It's not my desire here to replicate an already overloaded library shelf with such redundant pieces of wisdom. Instead I would like to concentrate on a single aspect of working alone at home; to spend some time helping you to decide if and when to leave your home office and rent outside space, a seemingly trivial, but actually a crucial step.

My beginning assumption is that you have acquired the support and encouragement of your spouse if you are married; of your parents or relatives if you are living with them; of your cohabitation partner if you are sharing your living quarters; or of your family and friends if you are living alone. (The first one that needs convincing support and encouragement is yourself, and I assume you've already seen to that.) We could make it easy and say that you've been laid off your job; but instead, let's suppose the decision to go off on your own *was* your own. You resigned. You quit. You gave the boss the raspberry. You walked away. You had a plan to work alone, and you went and cut the umbilical cord; you burned all the bridges, and to boot, you tore down all the road signs. Your initial reaction is relief; the weight of the world has been lifted from your shoulders.

Then panic sets in. You begin to realize what you have done, and you point yourself home—home to the comforts of hearth and heart. Your first inclination is to crawl into bed, disappear under the covers, and attempt to convince yourself that you did *not* quit your job; that you did *not* tell the boss that he had the brains, competence, and talent of an overripened eggplant; that you did *none* of these things. You know terror. You pray that it has all been a bad dream and you will wake up, and when next Friday comes around you will have your old, regular, always-there-when-you-expected-it, biweekly pay check handed to you.

Nope. Sorry. Not so. It's real. You're on your own, and you've got you to thank for it. So get up and get going. From now on your income will be directly related to your own output. Your success will be be measured by the length of time you can keep going without recourse to borrowing money or taking another salaried position. Much of that success will depend upon if and for how long you occupy a home office. In many situations, and for many personal reasons, you simply have no choice, and will maintain a home office for as long as you are working alone. But in many cases you do have a choice. Here are the three categories and four rules that pertain to working alone in your home:

(A) *You work at home when*
   (1) You have defined an office space totally apart from the rest of the house; you don't know if anyone else is home, and they don't know if you are in your office.
   (2) You write copy, review books, draw cartoons, or are engaged in similar endeavors where your new work activity does not involve outsiders coming to visit you in your office.
   (3) You are the only adult in the house during the work day.
   (4) There are no children living with you.
(B) *You consider moving to an outside office when*
   (1) The only office space you can use in your home

is not totally isolated from the rest of the house; you can clearly hear the television pounding away in the next room.

(2) Your new work activity involves occasional visits to your office by outsiders.

(3) Your spouse/house-mate spends some of the work day at home

(4) You have children over age 18 in the house.

(C) *You make immediate plans to move your office away from your home if*

(1) Your office actually shares space with another functional room in your home; i.e., it is physically a part of your kitchen or family room.

(2) You are, say, a marriage counselor or computer repair-person, and your new work activity involves regular visits to your home office by outsiders.

(3) Your spouse/house-mate spends most of the working day at home.

(4) You have children under age 18 in the house.

(*Special Note*: If you have preschool-aged children in the house, go directly from the job you quit to a real estate agent and rent office space. Do this even before you go home and perform the "crawl into bed" ritual.

I urge you to respect the somberness with which I present these guidelines. If at all possible, follow them. The informality and comfort afforded by an office at home can soon (very soon) evaporate into a dismal cacophony of antipathy, acrimony, and animosity as the flow of life of a "normal" household comes into conflict with the demands of an "abnormal" workplace.

You have placed an enormous strain upon yourself and your loved ones by leaving a well-paying job to strike out on your own. It behooves you to not add to that tension by creating a lose-lose situation at home. You owe it to those closest to you to shield them, to every extent possible, from the consequences resulting from your change in career. At the very best, that change will be transparent to them, and in terms of goods and services provided by you, they will be unaffected by the change. Realistically, though, you must expect a transition interval that carries with it periods of some regret and perhaps some hardship. But by planning that transition interval carefully, you can mitigate some of these early hardships. One of the quickest ways to do that is, if you find yourself firmly ensconced in category (C) above, to get office space outside of your home as soon as possible.

55 | FOURTH AND 99

Don't punt—try the end around

In the 1960s the University of Texas initiated, under its then football coach, an academic tutoring system for its student athletes that has since been adopted by many of our colleges and universities. Under that system a "brain coach," carrying the full credentials of any assistant coach in the athletic department, was hired and given the responsibility for maintaining a sufficient level of academic competence among the "jocks" to assure their remaining eligible for interscholastic competition. The brain coach, in turn, hired (at reasonable wages) a cadre of graduate students from the various academic disciplines to do the actual tutoring. I was hired as the geology tutor and spent three evenings a week one-on-one with a remarkable crew of youngsters. I helped them get through their required geology courses, and they helped me put together a set of memories on which I still draw to illustrate a particular point I am making. The following is just such an example.

When you have made your decision and commitment to work alone, there will be a period of euphoria that will carry you for a substantial time. It will take you through the difficult transition period from your salaried past to your entrepreneurial future. It may even carry you beyond the planning stage into the actual implementation phase of your new activities. But eventually—and it happens to everyone more than once—self-doubts begin to creep in. You fight these doubts, of course. You wouldn't be where you are now if you were the sort of person who simply folded up his pushcart at the slightest sign of rain. But gnawing doubts have a hardness beyond that of diamond, and by exerting formidable pressure they are able to penetrate even the strongest mental armor.

I can't tell you precisely and exactly what your own defense/response should be; I can only tell you how I handle the situation. Oh, yes indeed. It still happens to me every now and then. I recognize the early symptoms. It starts when I find myself "sleeping in." I'm usually up and about by 5:00 A.M. If, two or three days running, I find myself pulling the covers over my head at 6:00 or 7:00 A.M., it's a sure sign I'm turning a corner and about to run smack into a brick wall of self-doubt, concerned about what the future will bring. For the past several years, whenever that happens, I stare up at the ceiling, turn on the mental computer, click on MacMemory, and open the Bill Jones folder. Bill Jones isn't his real name, but if he reads this and recognizes himself, as he will, I know he won't mind my sharing his story with you. I hope MacMemory does him sufficient justice.

Bill came into my evening tutoring class as a relaxed and confident freshman. He was friendly and smiled gregariously. He stood about six feet three inches and possessed all the necessary attributes of a Texas high school football star. He was realizing and fulfilling a boyhood dream of playing varsity football in Memorial Stadium at the University of Texas. He came from a successful ranching family in a neighboring Texas county, and began playing football as a youngster. Now, at the ripe old age of eighteen, after having devoted his physical and intellectual life to that sport, football was the *sine qua non* of his being.

He was a quick learner, and made my tutoring task for his freshman geology course almost unnecessary. He appeared regularly through September and October, then didn't show up at all for several weeks. One day in December, he walked into the room a totally different person. His arms—both arms—were in casts from the wrists to the shoulders. He was sullen and withdrawn. His grades had taken a tailspin. These were obviously bad times. It took a while to get him to say anything, and when he did respond, it was in muttered, short sentences and reluctant monosyllables. As I pasted the story together, it seemed that Bill had inadvertently been flirting with disaster by playing football all those years. A routine physical examination had uncovered a weakness in his bone structure, including hairline fractures in both arms—serious only if Bill continued his football career. Otherwise the problem was healable and insignificant. The medical prognosis was clear and the decision was already made for him. No football. Ever again. Anywhere. Period.

He stayed awhile. I was doing most of the talking, never sure if he was listening. It's difficult to convince an eighteen-year old of your own wisdom; I was barely ten years older than he. But I attempted to assure him that the world had not ended, that the future indeed held promises yet to be fulfilled, challenges yet to be undertaken, victories yet to be tasted. When he left, he left quietly, and like Omar Khayam, " . . . came out the same door that in he went." In the years that followed, I wondered every now and then what had become of Bill Jones.

Now, a change of scene. It's the early 1980s, some twenty years later. My wife and I are attending a University of Texas-Exes social gathering on Capitol Hill, and a strangely familiar figure is walking briskly towards me, smiling, hand outstretched, with a lovely lady in tow. My wife spots him first, and while he's still out of hearing range, whispers, "Who's that coming at us?" Out of the corner of my mouth I say, "I don't know." But even as I say that, the memory of that Texas evening so many years ago comes flooding back, and when he grabs my hand and says, "Howdy Murray, great to see you again," I say, without having to look at his name tag, "Howdy Bill, it's been a while, how've you been?"

Following wive-ly introductions, we brought each other up to date on our activities. Bill had indeed stopped playing football. He had graduated, and gone on to take his law degree at the University of Texas. He was now serving as administrative assistant to a U.S. senator (from Texas, of course), and was planning his own run for Congress. Since then, Bill indeed ran for a seat in the U.S. Congress from his home district, won that seat, and eventually worked his way up to Deputy Minority Whip of the U.S. House of Representatives. He left Washington to make a run for governor of Texas, and lost that bid. He's now practicing law in Texas, and I suspect we Washingtonians haven't seen the last of him.

So whenever I get my own set of heebie-jeebies, depression, and blues, worrying about the future, I pull myself out of bed and find an 8″ × 10″ photo I keep around. It's got me sitting in a U.S. congressman's chair, at his desk in the Longworth House Office Building. The congressman is standing beside me with his arm on my shoulder, and we're both grinning broadly. Neither of us is thinking football.

56 | D.C. DELIGHT

Show time: putting my money where my mouth is . . .

Well, I guess I owe you a little bit extra if you've gotten this far in the book. I mean, you've obviously absorbed and enjoyed much of what I've said, or you wouldn't have reached this page. As a reward for you, and as a little prod to me, I've decided to put myself on the line and tell you about something I'm now doing, the outcome of which I am not at all sure of.

One of the good things about working alone—as you know by now—is that if the whim strikes you and time and resources are available, you are able to initiate any new kind of money-making activity you desire. Two weeks ago I had the appropriate combination of time, resources, and whim to put together a small package of essays I am sending out to one hundred newspapers around the country. I am proposing to write a weekly column for them dealing with the foibles of the federal bureaucracy. I am calling the column, "D.C. Delight," and I'm using the pen name "G. S. Wunn." You will remember that federal government service (G.S.) is ranked from G.S.-1 through G.S.-15, with each G.S. rank divided into ten steps. (In the olden days there were "supergrades" G.S.-16 through G.S.-18, but these have been replaced with the Senior Executive Service [SES]). At any rate, I've adopted the G.S.-1 federal employee, the lowliest of the low, called him G. S. Wunn, and given him authorship of D.C. Delight. What I will now do is to go through, with you, the actual mechanics

161

of starting D.C. Delight, my creative "something," out of
virtual zero. My rationalization for undertaking this new
venture is that it won't cost too much to test it out, and if
it works it will make some money. If it fails, then I can say
I had fun trying something new, and I still have a bunch of
essays I can one day use somewhere else. So here goes.

The first thing I did was to outline what it was I wanted
to do. I did this in the form of a cover memorandum to
prospective newspaper editors. I planned the memorandum
as a two-pager; the first page to be used as an introduction to
the concept, a reason for undertaking it, and a presentation
of my own applicable credentials. After several drafts I was
finally satisfied with the following:

D.C. DELIGHT
By G. S. Wunn
(pen-name of Dr. Murray Felsher)
1057-B National Press Building
Washington DC 20045

Memorandum: (Date)
To: Editorial Staff
From: DR. MURRAY FELSHER
Subject: D.C. DELIGHT

The past year has focused even more than the usual
attention on Washington D.C.—its politicians, foibles,
and flaps. Undoubtedly, this upcoming year promises
to continue, and most likely enhance the nation's interest in this little town of our's. We continually receive,
like Manna from Heaven, even more bushels of grist
for our humor mill, in the form of political appointees,
congressmen, staffers, and lobbyists, et al. who come and
go (many though, come and stay).

And at the nucleus of the ephemeral turmoil and incon-
stancy that is the hallmark of our nation's capital, we
find that one institution that assures our country's con-
tinuity and governmental consistency. That institution is
the Federal Bureaucracy (bless its stifled soul), and it is

that institution which forms the basis of D.C. DELIGHT, a column I wish to see in your newspaper.

I am one of those who "came and stayed." I once was a professor at a prestigious university in upper New York State, and came to Washington D.C. in 1969 for a short two-year stint helping run a National Science Foundation-funded college curriculum development program. I came down with a terminal case of Potomac Fever and joined the headquarters offices of the newly-formed Environmental Protection Agency, eventually transferring to the National Aeronautics and Space Administration headquarters. I spent ten years as a senior scientist in both agencies, and left the federal establishment (but not the federal city) in 1980. Since that time I have been publishing newsletters (two are *Washington Remote Sensing Letter*, reporting on applications of satellite photography of the Earth; and *Washington Federal Science Newsletter*, reporting on scientific and technical activities of all federal agencies). As such I have kept in close touch with my friends in the federal arena, and have looked forward to a future where I would write a column about their strange and wonderful existence. "The future," as a local football coach used to say, "is now."

Okay. That's page one. It tells the editor a little bit about what I propose to write about, and a little bit about me. Just as important, it lays out my writing style for all to see, and that alone will immediately turn on or turn off a prospective subscriber. I'm not afraid of that. Indeed, I'd rather have both us know, as soon as possible, if my writing style is appropriate, because I'm not going to change it. Now for page two of the cover memorandum. Here I present the specifics, terms and conditions, rates, and subscription form:

I have enclosed five pieces (four regular columns, plus a one-time bonus), to serve as your initial columns, and propose to send you four additional columns of about the same size (circa 500 words), at the beginning of each month. Payment will be made quarterly; a subscription form/invoice is included below to cover this quarter. Rate is $120.00 per quarter. That comes to $10.00 per column for the 12 columns provided in each 3-month period, (2.0 cents per word). As an added inducement, I am offering a one-time initial annual subscription rate of $420.00 per year (four quarters). Right is granted for single publication of each column within the month received; all other rights are reserved. Columns must show "G. S. Wunn" byline. G. S. Wunn is the pen-name of the column's author, Murray Felsher. *Authorized signature/title below is your acceptance of these terms and conditions. Form must be signed.*

Yes, I know these are hard times. But hard times often call for a good laugh, and I think you'll appreciate what you see here. I do think we have a winner—for both of us. Please complete the form below, and send in this entire sheet with your check. I do look forward to welcoming you as a subscriber to D.C. DELIGHT.

RETURN THIS ENTIRE SHEET
WITH YOUR CHECK
Editorial Offices: 1057-B National Press Bldg. Washington DC 20045,

Please sign me up for *D.C. DELIGHT*

I am enclosing: ___ **$120.00 for a 3-month subscrip-**
(Check one)   **tion** (January 1, 1994–31 March 1994)

___ **$420.00 for an annual subscrip-**
tion (January 1, 1994–31 December 1994)

Send *D.C. DELIGHT* to:
Name _____
Address _____

_____
_____ Zip _____ Date _____

Authorized Signature/Title _____

Return Page and Check to:
D.C. DELIGHT
P.O. Box 2075
Washington DC 20013

So much for page two. You may wonder how I arrived at the subscription rates cited above. Well, I tried to get to a reasonable-sounding "quarterly" number, and one that wouldn't be outrageous when multiplied by four as an annual rate. Further, by translating down to "cents-per-word," the rate would look downright cheap. We'll see if it works.

As you note from page two, I wrote five *D.C. Delight* essays and included them with the package I sent to the one hundred newspapers. That was a necessity. I don't know how many will subscribe, based on the five essays I enclosed, but I know that none would subscribe without an actual example of the goods for which they were paying. Two of the five are replicated below; the first:

D.C. DELIGHT:
by
G. S. Wunn

1. You're Right. We're Wrong . . .
   Now, let's suppose that The Boss informs you that the U.S. Congress had the temerity to have its Office of Technology Assessment (OTA) empanel a group of experts to review your pet program and pass judgment on the Way-You-Do-Business. An awesome prospect! Is it time to panic? No. Not to worry. Listed below are the

basic rules for turning around such a potential piece of *mal-de-mind* into a bureaucratic boon.

(1) Agree with The Boss that your program is in dire need of a critical review. Never, never argue this point. The key phrase in your initial response is, " . . . I have always felt that our program has suffered from a lack of outside peer evaluation." Never mind that your recent Memo To The File* noting your conversation with Dr. What's-His-Name from the University of Where-With-All pointed out that he had better keep his pointed head out of your program or you'll bounce him from your Advisory Committee, and he can kiss bye-bye to his $300 per day stipend and those quarterly trips to Washington.**

(2) You will be asked to review your program for the panel. Be certain that the actual presentation is made by one of your subordinates. What he says is unimportant. It is essential, though, that the subordinate (male or female, it makes no difference) be immaculately dressed, nails manicured, shoes shined, and teeth sparkling white—as befits a human sacrifice. At each point in the presentation whenever you detect unease, unrest, or dissatisfaction on the part of the panel, you must look surprised, shake your head slowly back and forth, and silently glare at the presenter. After the third or fourth time, start making clucking sounds with your tongue—barely audible at first, and then progressively louder and louder as the presentation rolls on. Precisely five minutes before the presentation is due to end, lean back in your chair, fold your hands behind your neck, stare at the ceiling and quietly hum. At exactly one minute before the presentation ends, stand up and leave the room without saying a word or looking at anyone. You have thus succeeded in disengaging yourself, in the eyes of the panel, from having had any connection whatsoever with your own program!

*See D.C. Delight No. 4, *"Dear Mr. Cabinet . . ."*
**See D.C. Delight No. 21, *Experts and Consultants: Which are Which?*

(3) Return directly to your office and shoot off a memo to The Boss, indicating your dismay at the state of your program and suggesting reassignment of the presenter.

(4) When the panel reports out its results, which will be devastating, send the panel chairman a long, personal letter. Most of what you write to him is of no consequence, as long as the very last paragraph says, *exactly*:

" . . . We agree wholeheartedly with your conclusion that our management methodology and technical protocol are misleading and of questionable worth. Further, your comment regarding the inapplicability of our results to real-world situations is an accurate assessment. Your remarks concerning our general ineptness were appreciated. Your presumption as to the shallowness of our approach was perceptive. We agree totally with all of your conclusions, and will continue to study your report in depth. Please be aware that we have submitted, in our next year's budget, an expanded program designed to rectify the situation as you so vividly portrayed it. To that end, I believe that the 200 percent increase in funding sought, and the 7 additional staff members I have requested will go far in alleviating your concerns. We have enjoyed working with your panel, and look forward to hearing from you again."

And the second:

D.C. DELIGHT:
by
G. S. Wunn

5. *The Staff Meeting: Looking Good For Zipper**
There are six professionals on the Boss's immediate staff counting you, Manfred Zipper. The weekly staff meeting, scheduled each Thursday at 10:00 a.m. is now 30 minutes old, and a co-staffer, Ethyl Graffbilder, is

---

*See D.C. Delight No. 14, *The Staff Meeting: Sam, You Made the Charts Too Long*.

briefing her way up a statistically insignificant road with no standard deviation, she having already drowned everyone present in a sea of chi-squares, F-tests, and rank correlations. It is obvious that The Boss is uninterested; witness his yawns which started out as barely-suppressed, and have now reached the point of being hardly muffled cataclysmic " . . . Yyy-ahrrrrs," booming out every 54 seconds. You, of course, are totally incompetent when it comes to statistical matters. You wouldn't know a regression line from a clothes line, and a table of random numbers would serve you not at all, save for helping you make obscene telephone calls. Sitting there, pretending to listen hard, you feel yourself shifting into an operational mode to take advantage of (A) the Boss's clear expressions of boredom; and (B) your own ignorance of the subject matter being presented, but your profound understanding of its ABCs (Appropriate Buzzword Constructs). You sense that you can walk out of this meeting Looking Good.

Let's watch carefully and see how it's done. Pay particular attention to Manfred's technique and timing, as well as the syntax of his comments and questions. Take notes and please hold your own questions to the end:

Graffbilder: . . . and as the square root increases to Point B in Chart two, note that the number of pages per report varies in proportion to the cube of the number of letters in the senior author's surname. This becomes significant at the 0.05 percent level, and may be directly correlated with an R-square of 0.94, assuming . . .

The Boss: . . . Yyy-ahhhrrrr!

Zipper: Excuse me, Ethyl.

Graffbilder: Yes, Manfred?

Zipper: Ethyl, do I understand you correctly? Are you saying that we are dealing with a non-normal distribution?

Graffbilder: No, it's definitely a *normal* distribution.

Zipper: Assuming that you're wrong, how do you explain your rejection of the Null Hypothesis?

Graffbilder: What?

Zipper: Well, I mean, let's assume that your hypothesis is incorrect. Everything then fits into place very well.

The Boss: . . . Yyy-ahhrrrr!

Graffbilder: (Glaring at Zipper) Continuing on. We can show . . .

Zipper: Excuse me, Ethyl. I still don't accept your primary Given. Let me suggest a way out of your dilemma . . .

Graffbilder: (In confusion) I *have* no dilemma!

Zipper: Assuming you do . . .

Graffbilder: (In anger) I don't!

Zipper: But for the sake of reaching a valid plateau, let's say I'm right and you're wrong. Your basic relationship then is not one of cause-effect, but rather it is associative, not so?

Graffbilder: (In panic) What the hell are you talking about?

Zipper: I'm glad you agree with me, Ethyl. (Turning to The Boss) Boss, I think we should go on record as uncommitted on this one. It's still got too many fuzzies hanging out of it.

Graffbilder: (In defeat) What the hell is he talking about?

The Boss: Well, let's break this up. Ethyl, see me in my office, will you? (Turning to Zipper) Manfred, that was a clear-headed analysis, good work!

(Exeunt)

I got out a copy of the *Editor and Publisher Yearbook,* which lists all you'll ever want to know about every newspaper in the country, and selected one hundred dailies to which I sent my packages. Actual total time spent: fourteen hours. Actual total money spent: forty-six dollars, including postage. And that's that. I don't know what will come of these. You may or you may not see them in your local newspaper.

GIGS, GUILT,
AND GREED

It's never too late to go back and get your
law degree

Not long after leaving federal employ, I was asked to
deliver an "extended lecture," or "short short-course," at
a large state university. I'd rather not specify its location,
though you might know it from my little story to follow. My
lecture was to be part of an environmental sciences course
being offered to a group of undergraduates, and it dealt with
a case I had been involved with in southern Florida while
I was with the Environmental Protection Agency. I have
always enjoyed lecturing on satellite remote sensing applications to environmental problems, and looked forward to
the session.

In fact, this university was no more than twenty miles
from the site of an old hazardous waste dump site, which
had become one of the country's most devastating environmental problems. The students would be well aware of
that local (but nationally prominent) condition, and would
be paying particular attention to my lecture, I was certain.
The lecture request came from the course professor, who
had been a participant in an environmental short course I
had taught a year or two earlier. He offered to pay my
expenses, which I accepted, and he offered an honorarium,
which I declined.

In one of those strange coincidences that remain inexpli-
cable, I received a phone call, seeking consulting assistance,
two days before I was to leave for the lecture. The call came
from an officer of the very same company responsible for

dumping the hazardous waste and creating the local disaster noted above. The caller, a corporate vice-president, wanted to know if satellite imagery could be used to show that no environmental damage could be attributed to the waste deposited at that site by the company. I told him I'd be back to him shortly, and hung up.

I felt an immediate twinge. Here I was, going to lecture a group of college students about the use of space-derived imagery to mitigate "environmental insults" (a term that isn't used much anymore, but we used it a lot then), wearing my white hat. At the same time, literally, I would be helping a large company prepare to defend itself against similar charges using that very same space technology. I thought about it long and hard. And the more I thought about it, the more distressed I felt. I argued to myself that all I would be doing was presenting the facts, letting them fall where they would—very much like any good attorney would do. Then I argued to myself that no self-respecting EPA-trained lawyer would go private and try to justify the actions of such a company, and defend its awful environmental record. (Hey, I was just starting out on my own, and still a bit naive.) But I was looking for work, and finally, overcome by greed, and accompanied by a mental suitcase full of rationalizations, I called back and agreed to take the job. It was to be a one-day briefing. It turned out to be a one-hour briefing, since all I could show them was imagery which could only be used to support both the government's case and public interest groups' claims against the company. I charged them $700 for my one-hour talk.

That was many years ago, but I thought about it often, picturing myself going directly from classroom to board-room, trading in my white hat for a black hat, so to speak, collecting a few dollars, and feeling pangs of guilt. That is, until this morning. Now I'm just feeling dumb.

Today at 5:49 A.M. I was tooling down Canal Road on the way to my newsletter office, and listening to our local public radio station. (You must know that I'm not a public radio/classical music snob. The 'Vette radio has but four FM buttons, and I have them set to classical, light rock, country, and rock & roll—my tastes in music pretty much replicate my tastes in life, namely, if it doesn't hurt, it's good for you, but opera still hurts me.) Anyway, I was listening to the "Environmental Minute," as they call it, and I heard mentioned the name of a prominent lawyer. He and I served at EPA together, and I provided technical support to several major environmental cases he pursued there. He was the most environmentally-conscious individual I had ever met—eager to do battle with any corporate ogre who would befoul the environment. He was smart and he was audacious. And I was certain he stayed that way after leaving EPA.

The radio announcement was that the government's longest and most expensive environmental case had just ended, with the judge expected to take a full year to sift through the volumes of evidence presented by both sides. The case was that same one I had felt so "twingey" about. And the chief attorney for the company was my old friend from EPA. I'm betting he's charging something more than $700.

Maybe it's not too late to go back and get my law degree.

58 THE "GREAT MAN" THEORY

Do it if you can

To successfully work alone you have to be a true believer in the "great man" theory. If it bothers you, then for "man" you can substitute "woman," or "person." Further, if it still bothers you, please understand that I don't impute to myself any sense of "greatness." It's only a phrase. If you've gotten this far in the book, you've already come across enough graphic instances that will confirm for both of us that "me" and "great" are mutually exclusive. Good, maybe, but not great. . . .

In an earlier piece I spoke of humanity's normal curve as it relates to our assertive creativity. When I speak of the great man theory, I again refer to that normal curve, but in a still more harsh fashion. What follows is the "macro-picture":

I maintain that events and circumstances of our being, and the very fabric of our lives, are the results of actions cast into motion, nonconspiratorially, by single individuals—sometimes separated from us by many miles and many years. The ebb and flow of everything from social conduct to moral interaction to legal obligation is but a consequence of decisions taken by individuals who, by dint of their economic or political stature, and with or without our consent, are provided with power, and use that power to influence, dictate to, and otherwise move the masses. (This power has been enhanced enormously in our present technological era. The current "information age" will place

174

a frightening amount of power into the hands of a very few highly placed individuals attached to massive organizations: secular institutions such as governments and corporations, as well as religious institutions. This can be a harbinger of either infinite good or incredible evil.)

Civilization, any civilization, is but a resulting footnote to these individual decisions. We may call it "history," but history is a moving picture, ever-changing, that responds in real time to decisions and events continually being created by great men. The present, then, is nothing but a crude snapshot, providing an instantaneous recording of the current state. The future? The future does not exist, and never does exist. (Heavy words. Read 'em again.) So much for the "macropicture."

Now for the "micropicture": Within the framework just given, most of the people, most of the time, and most everywhere, are responding to events and decisions created by others. Again, think of that great normal curve. Think of that curve as it was described by ex-Astronaut Michael Collins in his spectacular book, *Carrying the Fire* (1974, p. 151), where he says, " . . . In between, inconspicuous under the dome of the bell-shaped curve, cowered the majority."

Cowered the majority! I like that. The essence of working alone is the very antithesis of cowering with the majority. To succeed alone you must do everything *but* cower with the majority. You must be free to both make decisions and boldly implement them. You take risks. You succeed, and take risks again to succeed again. You fail, and you take risks again to succeed the next time. You operate within allowable constraints imposed by legal mandates, limited by an obdurate bureaucracy, and are defined by your own moral standards. You thus create your own little world, always butting your head up against the boundaries of the envelope. But that provides you with the self-fulfillment that you require, and it is that which separates you from the "cowering majority" by light-years. No, you may never end up being a "great man," but you're good, yes you're good.

59 | A BASIC QUESTION

Security, where is thy blanket?

I have discovered, both by personal experience and by visiting with people who have stepped out on their own, that the single initial, and most important reason for wanting to work alone, is independence. That translates to a strong desire to seek freedom from fulfilling another's (generally your supervisor's) expectations. As a salaried person, you may reside comfortably under the corporate umbrella, accumulating all the benefits thereunto due you. But as penalty you carry an awful lot of baggage—some will say, "too much." And they will move out.

In my mind, a salaried position is to working alone as renting an apartment is to owning a house. In an apartment you are living in narrowly defined and *con*fined quarters. In a house you have room to grow and spread out. Further, in an apartment you are expending your efforts (paying rent) for someone else's benefit (reducing the landlord's mortgage, not to mention allowing him to deduct his interest payments at tax time). In your own home *you* are deriving the mortgage, tax, and investment benefits.

My basic question is, "Why in the world would anyone *not* want to work alone?"

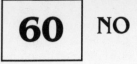

60 | NO

No—En, O—No. The infamous two-letter word

Back in the good old days, when I was young and gasoline was twenty-three cents a gallon (honest), I spent one summer working as a camp counselor. My high school credentials included membership on the swimming team, and that, together with an American Red Cross Lifesaving Certificate, was reason enough for the camp director to put me on the "convoy team." Our job was to swim next to the campers as they splashed through the water taking their beginner, intermediate, and advanced swimming tests, passage of which would allow them to swim in the deeper waters and to take boats and canoes out into the lake. It was good duty, especially on those hot, muggy days when my coworkers were teaching leather handicrafts and lanyard-making in sweaty non-airconditioned shacks.

Well, for some reason or another, an unexplainably high percentage of campers failed their tests when I was swimming convoy. More than half, in fact, would sputter and flail, and I would have to take them in tow, enduring their moans and curses, back to the dock. Word began to be passed around by the campers to " . . . avoid Felsher for convoy duty." (In my own defense, I go on record as stating that I believe, in many instances, we were dealing with a self-fulfilling prophecy, with campers failing because they *expected* to fail.)

Eventually, the epitasis reached its ruinous conclusion when the campers got together and petitioned the director to remove me from convoy duty, since I was clearly the reason so many of them were failing. The director, ignoring my rolling of the eyeballs skyward, and oblivious to my pointing out to him the *post hoc* fallacy, felt it his duty to take me out of the water and into the leather-craft shack. Leather wallets shaped like owl-heads, I do believe. I spent the rest of the summer dripping sweat instead of treading water.

My only reason for having you thus share my distant, but still perfect memory, is to point out a very important lesson that is well understood by prepubescent children of both sexes; yet, somehow, it is lost to so-called mature, intelligent adults of the same two sexes. The lesson is (1) if the guy is doing you wrong or (2) if you perceive him as doing you wrong, or (3) even if he has the potential for doing you wrong, then *lose the guy*.

As we grow older we become encumbered with an ever-increasing patina of social mores that prevents us from directly doing what we know is right. We engage in minor subterfuges, we tell little white lies, we construct massive towers of deception, all designed to prevent us from hurting someone's feelings, or to get us out of an obligation, or to provide us with an excuse not to face the truth. As comforting, rewarding, and acceptable as these ploys may be when you are on a salary, they are, each and every one, intolerable when you are working alone. To succeed alone you cannot afford to spend time in goal-less, unproductive, and meaningless activities. Granted, you might want to set aside a bit of time here or there to chew the fat, contemplate the *Starship Enterprise*, or play a computer game. But if these events become the cornerstone of your workday, then I have only this piece of advice; marry rich.

As you get better and better known, engaging in more and varied activities, you will be sought out by people. I'm not talking about potential clients; but those individuals who, for reasons of their own, wish to claim an hour or two of your time. They've read something you've written, they've heard you on a radio talk show. They've seen you on a panel at a professional society meeting. They want to go beyond a cursory chat and a handshake. They will call you on the phone or write long letters, and they will expect instantaneous, complete, and ongoing responses. Your answer, my friend, must be "no." A kind "no," perhaps, but "no" nonetheless. These phrases must become, unashamedly, a part of your repertoire:

"No, I'm sorry, I can't do that."

"No, I haven't the time to answer your letter."

"No, we can't meet for lunch."

"No, I couldn't possibly read your 900-page manuscript."

"No."

Note the first word of each sentence. Practice saying it. Now practice saying it like you mean it.

Having said all that, you may now perceive me as an unmitigated misanthrope. No, not so. (See how easy it is to say, "No?" Once you've gotten the hang of it, I assure you that it will become a mainstay of your vocabulary.) Having made my point, however heavily, I will back away slightly, and confess that it is an unusual person indeed who would permanently crawl, hermitlike, into his noncommunicative cave. So indeed, do reach out and touch someone every now and then, but save your best stuff for the paying customer.

And furthermore, it was *not* my fault that those kids failed their swimming tests—miserable brats. That leathercraft shack was hell!

61 | VILLA CAPRI

Remembrances

As you progress through life, you gather about you all sorts of things: some good, some bad, and some in between. However, if you are fortunate, you will accumulate three articles of supreme value. One of these is material goods, the acquisition of which forms the basis of the book you are now reading. But I am here to tell you that such goods are an anathema if they are obtained, assembled, and utilized in the vacuum of self-gratification. A major liability always facing me and any individual working alone is the risk of insulating and isolating oneself from the surrounding world. Recognizing that fact, I point out that the other two articles of supreme value you must never stop accumulating are (1) memories and (2) friends. In that context I offer the following recitation, which speaks to (1); I'll save (2) for later.

Memories can fulfill a special need, particularly if they travel across several temporal tracks, and can be pressed against events which form one's own "life markers." Such a reminiscence is the one that revolves about a now-razed motel in Austin, Texas, called the Villa Capri.

My wife and I arrived in Austin, Texas, in September 1961, as nearly newlyweds. I had completed my M.S. studies in June; She had gotten her B.S. a week earlier. Somewhere in between we had gotten married. We spent that first summer in a rented basement apartment of somebody's house on Pelham Parkway in the Bronx, waiting for September and our move to Texas. That first summer, I commuted to C.C.N.Y., teaching a freshman geology course. The 1950 Chevy I had picked up for $25 in Amherst the previous year was in far better shape than it looked, but I knew that I would bend to the pressure of parents and in-laws and junk the car for the trip to Texas. I ended up buying a new VW beetle for $1,585, which cleaned us out.

No one I knew had ever been to Texas. When we drove off, I looked back and saw my parents, my in-laws, and my brother and his wife waving with a resigned wistfulness. They were certain (I was certain) that we would fall off the edge of the world and would never be heard from again.

The trip west and south was joyful. But I almost rammed the first longhorn we'd ever seen as it crossed a state highway at sunset, outside Tyler, Texas. When we reached Austin, where I was to begin my doctoral studies at the University of Texas, we stayed at an old motel on I-35, just north of Capital Plaza.

Our drive down I-35 to the university the following morning took us past the Villa Capri Motel. It was then brand new and magnificent. Its location, abutting the university on the east, was ideal for us while we looked for an apartment, but of course we couldn't afford to stay there. We peeked into the restaurant and were awed by the vaulted ceilings and rich appointments. Of course we couldn't afford to eat there either.

My teaching assistantship and my wife's job as an elementary school teacher with the Austin Independent School District, enabled us to set aside some money, so that when June 1962 rolled around we would be able to celebrate our first wedding anniversary at the Villa Capri—in style. It was sumptuous; we spent two-week's food money on that meal, but it was worth it.

Our first two children were born in St. Davids Hospital, just up the block from the Villa Capri. Our daughter, our first-born (having now completed her Ph.D.), was born prematurely, and had to remain in an incubator for some time; we didn't hold her for two months. Between classes I would visit the hospital nursery, and then wander down Red River Street to the Villa Capri and sit at a table alongside one of the pools, and stare into the rippled water, and think, and pray.

Several years later, on the day before I defended my Ph.D. dissertation, I flew into Austin and spent a sleepless night, preparing myself for the following day's ordeal. When it was over I walked back to the Villa Capri and sat at that same table alongside the same pool, for a long time.

In the summer of 1983 I flew to Amarillo to pick up our older son, the other Austinite, who was just completing a stay at Philmont Scout Camp in New Mexico, and bussing home through Texas. He was entering his senior year in high school, in Maryland, and he wanted to enroll as a freshman engineering student at the University of Texas. I suggested that he (we) spend a week in Austin so that he could get to know the town and the school. We flew down to Austin and spent the week at the Villa Capri.

But by then the motel was already tired and old. I-35 had been converted to an elevated highway and the Villa Capri was huddled in the shadow of the Interstate, as if ashamed of its appearance and obvious neglect. The Hudson River piers beneath the West Side Highway (where I had once spent a summer as a dockhand unloading trucks onto barges) always gave me that same feeling.

I had, some time ago, enrolled as a Texas-Ex Life Member. Recently, in one of their publications, tucked into a small sidebar, in an out-of-the-way page was the note:

The Villa Capri will soon be demolished to make space for UT expansion. The University bought the motel in December after it closed because of monetary problems. Located just across the street from Sid Richardson Hall, it was an Austin landmark for three decades.

Perhaps it was the matter-of-fact finality of that declaration that set my mind back over the years. And as I retrieved pieces of my ephemeral life and pressed them against the stability of an Austin motel, I discovered that the memories turned out to be more lasting and more enduring than were the bricks and mortar of the Villa Capri.

62 | PROTOCOL

It has to be you, it has to be you . . .

Last month I stood in line outside the U.S. Post Office in the Pentagon, waiting to pay my annual fee for a post-office box I am renting there. That's right. When you're working alone you do everything by yourself (including paying postal fees). The box is my drop for mailed subscriptions to my third newsletter, *Defense Contract Awards (DCA)*, and I'll say more about that newsletter in another essay.

It was two weeks before Christmas, and knowing that there would thus be a long wait at the post office, I showed up early, hoping to get as close as possible to the front of the line. I arrived at 7:30 A.M. (the Pentagon branch opens at 8:00 A.M.) and found about ten people already waiting. Number-one person, a marine sergeant, leaned against the wall, some five feet across from the locked entrance to the post office, and the line had formed behind him. I joined the line, and watched it extend at something like an exponential rate. By 7:45 A.M. it had replicated itself as would a living organism, and had disappeared out of sight down the Pentagon's main concourse. Nearly everyone I could see on line wore a uniform, and I imagine even those few in mufti were military as well.

At 7:55 A.M. an Air Force full-bird colonel carrying a small package walked straight up to the locked post-office door. He rattled the knob, and finding it locked, muttered something under his breath. He then looked at his watch, and remarkably, instead of traipsing to the rear, looking for the back of the line, which by now was undoubtedly spilling into the Potomac, he resolutely planted himself directly in front of the door, thereby claiming dibs on the number-one space. This, in full sight and disregard of fifty or so people who could bear witness to his boorish display of social misconduct.

Well, as a native New Yorker, I felt certain I knew what would happen next. Without doubt, at least a dozen angry uniforms would, at any moment, spring out and instantly pound Colonel Mustard, with fists, into the floor tiles. Any moment now. Pretty soon. Here they come . . . Well? This was unreal. Quite unbelievable. The marine sergeant, whose place was usurped, was seriously engaged in examining his right thumbnail. Number 2 in line, a very large army captain was deliberately staring at his shoes. Number 3, an Air Force major, was placidly smiling at nothing. And so it went. Ten seconds passed. Thirty seconds passed. Finally, from a position some eight or ten people behind me, a voice boomed out, "Colonel, get your butt to the end of the line." Colonel Butt-in-ski, chest bedecked with ribbons galore, spun around and, face red with anger, shouted, "Who said that?" And then out stepped The Voice, an Air Force major general, two stars gleaming in the dawn's early light. "I did," he said, neither softly nor friendlylike. The colonel blustered something about not realizing we were in the "post-office line," and strutted away to a spontaneous whistling, by the rest of us, of the Lieutenant Kobe March.

Well, okay. It makes sense. The Air Force colonel felt secure in his expectation that he could get away with breaking into the line, because the odds were that no one brought up in the military of a lower rank than he would dare confront him. Further, the odds were in his favor that there was no general officer or admiral in that line, for it would have taken one of these to move him from that spot. Sure, he knew that anyone, even a lowly feather merchant like me, could insist on his moving to the back of the line, but he went with his institutional intuition that no one would. And he was right. Unfortunately for him, though, he was wrong about a general not being in line. An Air Force general, no less. I silently hoped that the general had noted the name-tag on the offending colonel as he strutted past.

Now, what does all that have to do with working alone? Well, it has *everything* to do with working alone. You see, those military folk standing in that line are integral parts of a large, stable, strong institution; no different in those characteristics than any corporation or university. One of the very positive attributes of any such large institution is its ability to respond to threatening situations. "It" protects "itself" and "its" employees from adversity (from both within and without) by promulgating and enforcing rules and regulations. For more serious infringements than line-breaking it employs legal counsel. An institution—any institution—is well armed, committed, and intrepid. It can go with ease and confidence in harm's way.

But those of us working alone lack these trappings of institutional comfort. We cannot depend on our legal department to inform us of our rights; we have no legal department. And we cannot depend upon our generals to chastise line-breakers; we have no generals, in fact, we have no line-breakers. In truth, and to paraphrase the inimitable Pogo, " . . . we have met our lawyers and generals, and they are *us*."

Life among the working-aloners is not a continually ripple-free pond. There will be times when you will confront adversity. As a consultant you may be made to feel threatened and intimidated by the vaunted edifice of your client's distinguished organization. After all, he has the might of his whole institution to pit against you. And all you have is you. But it's up to you and you alone to state your position, fight for your rights, demand what is coming to you, and insist upon equitable resolution and redress.

This means there are times that you will not come across as a nice guy. This means there are times that you will be irascible. This means there are times you will be angry. This means there are times some people will not like you. This means there are times you will be called arrogant or impudent or smug or conceited or impertinent or haughty. And this means that at times you will be all of these.

This means there are times you will have to undertake the equivalent of telling a colonel to move his butt to the back of the line. And if you are able to do this with impunity sprinkled with a bit of joy, and with no repentance whatsoever, then it also means that you stand a good chance to succeed working alone.

63 | "NEXT TIMES"

If it was a good idea when you thought of it, then it always will be

Suppose you have what you feel is a great idea. And suppose that you then invest your efforts and resources in pursuing that idea. And then suppose that the idea fails. For whatever reason. Kaplunk. Blop. It goes nowhere. What do you do? You actually have two choices, whose tenets are diametrically opposed. You can adopt choice A, which states, "Forget it forever. It was a good idea, but the world wasn't ready for it, and probably never will be." Or, you can follow choice B, which says, "Never forget anything forever. You've planted the seeds; now go away and do something else while they germinate."

I guess you know by now that I'm a germinator. That's a *ger*minator, not a *ter*minator. It is important that you remain receptive to ideas, all ideas. You must be willing to listen to little bells going off in your mind, and you mustn't fear your own intuitive responses to these little bells. This concept is best stated, believe it or not, in a phrase from the old rock song, "Year of the Cat," where we hear the protagonist described as " . . . walking down the street like Peter Lorre, contemplating a crime." Now of course, I am not advocating anything illegal, immoral, or fattening here. A more benign, as well as appropriate interpretation of these lyrics would apply here. When you work alone you've got to walk down the street with senses aware, always ready to make a move, yet patient enough to realize that full fruition of that move may not become apparent for years. Metaphors and cliches as "keeping many oars in the water," and "juggling several balls at one time," may be trite, but they are germane.

The idea is that at any one time you should be involved in as many activities as you may feel comfortable handling. Some may be in what we call a phase-one feasibility stage. Some may be in the final implementation stage. Some may be anywhere in between. Some may have short-range, near-real-time payback. Some may be far-field strategic gambles. Some may be anywhere in between. Some may be sure-fire payoffs. Some may be "seed-droppers" (activities with no immediate or apparent payoff). Some may be anywhere in between. Get it? And if you do something once and it doesn't work, that doesn't mean it won't work the next time. But you'll never know unless you try it again. I keep a box tucked away whose label reads, "Next Times." Ofttimes I retrieve "Next Times" many times before they click. Some haven't clicked yet, but they will.

64 | WHAT GOES 'ROUND, COMES 'ROUND

Birthing ideas

Most everybody has heard of land-grant colleges, which, beginning in the 1860s, were provided with continuing federal funding, and in return established great agricultural schools which, to this day, undertake the nation's basic research in all aspects of agriculture: from agronomy to soil science, from forestry to entomology, and from botany to genetic engineering. The success of America's westward migration and fulfillment of its "manifest destiny" is linked directly to the agricultural revolution spawned by the nation's land-grant-college system.

Now, I'm certain not as many of you have heard of our sea-grant colleges. The sea-grant-college system was established, using land-grant colleges as a model. The time was one hundred years later, and the American frontier had long since moved beyond the bounding coasts and had spilled into the world ocean. The federal government initiated, in the mid-twentieth century, the sea-grant-college system for much the same reasons as it gave for establishing land-grant colleges in the nineteenth century. The program was created to strengthen U.S. basic research, this time in the marine sciences, by designating a set of colleges and universities as sea-grant institutions. The program was placed originally into the National Science Foundation, and then moved into the National Oceanic and Atmospheric Administration, an agency of the Department of Commerce, where it now resides.

In 1975, when as a federal technocrat (that's nothing but a bureaucrat with a Ph.D. after his name), I had transferred from EPA to NASA, I invented and decided to promote a "*space*-grant-college" program. The country was then approaching, and was on the verge of penetrating, a whole new frontier. The space shuttle was just moving off the drawing boards, and the space station was no more than a foggy dream. Yet, I felt that this was the time to start a program that would fund colleges around the country to have them establish the infrastructure necessary to carry America into space in the twenty-first century. A space-grant-college program would provide continuous support of all aspects of research, training, and education in the aerospace sciences. This, in turn, would precipitate the solid industrial base from which the United States would emerge as a global leader in overall space research, applications, habitation, and exploration.

The head of NOAA's sea-grant-college program was a friend, and he was kind enough to support my efforts by documenting the "birth" of his sea-grant program. For six months, on my own, I prepared and delivered my briefing packages, slowly moving up the NASA headquarters food chain (that's bureaucrat-ise for "management ladder"). I briefed my boss and his boss and his boss and finally, the associate administrator, who was the line manager of NASA's applications programs. Everybody up the line supported the idea. At each step, as I received comments from my peers and bosses I fine-tuned my presentation, and by the time I reached the associate administrator I was confident that I would win support from the ultimate powers-that-be in the executive branch of government— the bean-counters at the Office of Management and Budget (OMB)—the president's "no" men. ("No" men, as opposed to "yes" men who sycophantically agree with everything the boss says, are hired to be the bad guys and say no to new programs emanating from executive departments and agencies.)

Of course, there are programs that the president and OMB do want to see initiated. These programs are put on a greased fast track. One way in which this system would work is that the responsible agency comes up with the program and officially moves it into the office of a friendly congressman or senator, who in turn drafts a bill containing that program. In such instances, OMB indicates no displeasure, congressional hearings are held and comments are incorporated into senate and house versions of the bill. The bill is read out of conference and enacted, funds are authorized, then appropriated, and the agency in question goes to work doing what it had wanted to do in the first place. But all this hinges on agreement by OMB. Without OMB's agreement, the agency in question will fight tooth and nail against any new program, even one that was initiated within that agency itself. This I found out the hard way.

A combination of hard work and good fortune had brought me to the offices of a U.S. senator who, back in the mid-seventies, was considered a major supporter of space-related programs. My immediate supervisor at NASA (an ex-astronaut) had convinced the senator's staff that the space-grant-college idea was one of the finest concepts ever thought of, next to sliced toast and peanut butter. Together, we drafted a bill, The Space Grant College Bill of 1976, that the senator, with appropriate fanfare, introduced to congress. Everybody in the world thought it was even better than sliced toast and peanut butter, and public hearings were scheduled to confirm the efficacy and importance of that program. Everybody, that is, except OMB. The bill called for an additional five million dollars in new money to be added to the upcoming NASA budget, and OMB refused to go along with that.

To make a sad story even sadder, what happened next so outraged me that it was the single push that got me looking for my life's work outside the federal bureaucracy. What happened was that OMB sent a letter to the NASA administrator (The Boss), instructing him to testify *against* the proposed space-grant-college bill at the upcoming congressional hearings. The administrator, whom I had briefed, and who was one of the major supporters of the space-grant-college concept, agreed to testify against the bill, and sent a memo cascading down the agency food chain seeking out the most knowledgeable person available to write his testimony. Guess who got the job to write congressional testimony *against* the very bill that he helped draft, and the program that he invented. That's right, *moi*. Of course I found an acceptable excuse not to write that testimony, but I still had to stand by and watch the space-grant-college bill sink into oblivion, and with it the program I felt was so necessary and vital to our nation's future in space.

That was the beginning of the end of Felsher, the federal paper-pusher. But it was not the end of the space-grant-college program. In keeping with the previous essay, "Next Times," a strange and wonderful thing happened along about 1989. It seems that one U.S. senator, Lloyd Bentsen (D-TX), introduced something called a Space Grant College Bill, and it was enacted into law. NASA, for its part, established the program, funded it completely, and has supported it to the extent that there are now more than thirty funded and recognized space-grant college and university consortia operating in the United States. I must tell you that no one on the senator's staff or in the NASA program office had ever contacted me, spoke to me, or heard of me. In fact, when I presented myself to NASA's Space Grant College Program headquarters office, I was eagerly passed around from person to person, and was asked to fill in the details I have outlined above, relating to them my 1970s' initial "seed drop" of which they were totally unaware. I did receive a number of pats on the back, for which I was grateful. The full story, I suspect, will never be known. But someone, somehow, must have used my earlier work to get from then to now, and I am grateful for that.

Further, and more to the point, I am not at all hesitant in claiming credit for the concept, and expect to derive some meaningful income from NASA's Space Grant College Program office. We consultants, though we appreciate federal pats on the back, do require federal money in the bank.

NORTHERN EXPOSURE

Trust yourself

There is an old science-fiction story whose title I've long since forgotten, and whose author I never knew. The plot was intricate and complicated, and the only part I remember was but a footnote that described a NASA engineer who had rigged a special device aboard an unmanned rocket that was scheduled to impact the moon. (The moon-impact rockets were launched in the early sixties as part of the Ranger program, so I guess that dates the story a bit for those of you who want to track it down.) The engineer devised a pyrotechnic contrivance that caused an enormous replicate of the logo of a famous cola drink to be displayed above the moon's surface when the rocket impacted. The picture flashed around the world and was an incredible advertising coup. It was quickly noted that the engineer was summarily fired from his job, but the author surmised that he had been paid a sufficient sum of money by the soft-drink company to assure him and his descendents a comfortable life ever after.

I've already discussed the fact that a consultant has to be very careful, because all he has in his stockpile of knowledge and information is dross if it is compromised by a lack of personal and professional integrity. Unfortunately, that fictional NASA engineer has his counterparts in the consulting world. And indeed there are some individuals who will bend and twist the truth in order to satisfy the requirements of their clients, as well as assure themselves of further work with those clients. I have seen several blatant examples of this, and include one "fr'instance," when I was an almost-victim, to point out to you the care with which you must approach your own work. The fellow involved has since left the consulting business, and I have not heard his name mentioned for several years. Nonetheless, I am going to change several vital points of the story I am about to tell you, so that you will not be able to identify him or his company. He still might be a bit vindictive, as I think he knows I played a substantial part in his downfall.

This is about an environmental suit brought by the federal government against a major manufacturer in the northern Rockies. The case was one of the largest in the history of the Environmental Protection Agency, and I was hired as an expert witness by the government in its effort to stem the pollution emanating from a manufacturing process being undertaken by the company. The process was a beneficiation activity that took natural rock material and concentrated a specific mineral in that rock. The rock was brought in by rail as ore from a mine some seventy miles away. The beneficiation process itself resulted in a dry powder, and the process, though nonchemical in nature, did serve to concentrate the mineral in question. But unfortunately, the concentration process also released into a proximal lake, and, as part of the tailings' waste stream, a suite of minerals considered to be carcinogenic. The closest town, some forty miles away, derived its drinking water from that lake, and the EPA argued that the lake currents were bringing the carcinogenic minerals into people's kitchen faucets. The company argued that the material was a "natural" mineral, always present in streams that drained into the lake, and it would therefore be impossible to differentiate a carcinogenic mineral that originated in a natural stream from one that originated from the company's beneficiation activity.

Two things were very quickly apparent to me. First, even a casual reading of the local geological maps and reports showed that the mine from which the ore was shipped to the plant was located in an area which was drained by streams

belonging to an entirely different watershed than that occupied by the lake in question. In other words, streams that
fed the lake did not come from the mine area. Further, and
even more significant, that particular carcinogenic mineral
was located nowhere else in the area; only within the ore
body being mined by that company.

In order to prove that the minerals in the lake did indeed
come from the company, and *only* the company, we had to
show that the streams feeding into the lake contained no
such mineral suite, either as suspended material or in the
bed load. A team of us drove along the single, ice-patched
(it was early winter), two-lane road that paralleled the lake,
between the town and the plant, and whenever we came
to a bridge over a stream feeding the lake, we walked
upstream, away from the lake, taking samples as we went.
Our analysis, and the report we prepared for EPA, was no
surprise. The mineral in question simply was not present.
Period. This was a major finding for the government, and
placed in jeopardy the company's entire case.

Imagine my shock and surprise then, when a couple of
weeks later, I received a panic call from the Justice Department lawyer handling the case for EPA. At his insistence I
rushed over to his office and was handed a report prepared
by a private consultant hired by the company, that showed
emphatically, and without doubt, that the streams feeding
the lake between the town and the plant were bursting with
this mineral! Filled with dismay, I took the report to the
next room and read it from cover to cover.

There was no question about it. The stuff was there. That
is, unless you would accuse the consultant hired by the
company of actually fabricating the data. I wasn't prepared
to do that, even though I knew his findings were patently
wrong. Yet it placed the government's case in a most
awkward position, and the Justice Department was faced
with its own expert witness (me) having a vital piece of
testimony canceled out by the company's expert witness.
The whole strategy of the case would have to be shifted,
and the lawyer was gathering his staff for a planning session
as I walked back into his office. I had been serving as a

technical consultant to lawyers for years, and so I feel comfortable working with them. But I admit that I was not prepared for a room full of attorneys staring at me accusingly; it did make the sweat beads stand out on my forehead. Before anyone could speak, I said, "Look, I've put my own reputation on the line here. I *know* that I'm right and this guy is wrong. Give me twenty-four hours to go over his report in detail." No, I was told. The whole case has to be permutated. You've got till close-of-business today to show us that our consultant is better than their consultant.

Well, I thought, that gives me three hours. Three hours to figure out how so basic a measurement as a water and a mineral analysis could produce such different results by two consultants. Well, I concluded, they couldn't, unless one of them was lying outright; but I still couldn't accept the proposition that the other guy falsified his results. After all, it would be so easy to catch him at it. The actual samples were evidence in a federal court suit. We could re-analyze the same samples. No, I thought, I must assume that the analyses were accurate. If necessary, I could always return to the very same sample points and recover additional samples for analysis. Let's see exactly where they were taken. . . . I stopped, smiled, made a single long-distance telephone call, and walked back to the lawyers no more than fifteen minutes after I had left them. I started off by telling them that their consultant was better than the company's consultant, and that I expected the government to come up with a bonus. (No, government agencies do not give out bonuses to consultants.)

I stepped up to the easel in front of the room and drew two boxes connected by a line. One box was the town, the other the plant, and the line was the road we traveled between the two. Parallel to the road, I drew a line indicating the lakeshore, and feeding into the lake I drew several streams, as lines perpendicular to, and crossing the road. I then drew in several X'es showing locations of the samples I had taken, all of which contained no evidence of the mineral in question. The X'es were all upstream from the road, with none between the road and the lake. I then informed them that I believed the analyses indicated by the company consultant were *correct*, which drew a gasp from the assembled lawyers. I then placed a series of O's indicating where the company consultant had taken *his* samples. The O's were bunched, in all cases, *downstream* from the road, always between the road and the lake. I stopped. I looked at the lawyers. Nothing. "Well," I said. "Don't you see?" No they didn't.

Okay. It might not have been fair. But they *were* ready to hang me a few minutes earlier. I let them squirm for a bit, then told them that I had confirmed, by my long-distance call to the town's snow-removal authority, that the road between the town and the plant is regularly plowed, and further, that *some of the dry powder exiting the plant's beneficiation process is always donated by the plant and used to "salt" the roadway!* Boom. There it was. Passing vehicles, rain, and mamma nature wash the "salt" off the road. It makes its way to the streams below, and gets washed into the lake. So of course in the wintertime, each stream between the road and the lake (never upstream from the road), and all streams between the town and the plant (and no other streams feeding the lake) will be full of the carcinogenic mineral-rich "salt." And all of it comes from the company's tailing piles. And none of it is due to natural erosion and drainage of the ore body itself.

Now, I don't know what that consultant got in terms of a fee. However big it was, it wasn't worth it; his reputation and company disappeared simultaneously. As for me, I didn't get a bonus, but I did get a standing ovation from a room full of lawyers, and oh, yes . . . the government won the case.

Sometimes, to stand up for yourself you have to remain seated

There's a big difference between being "easygoing" and being taken advantage of. Somewhere between 1965 and 1990 I learned that difference, and acted on it. I'm not saying that it took a quarter of a century for me to become comfortably assertive; but I'm not sure if it was a gradual change or if I woke up one day and realized that you could be assertive and *still* be an easygoing guy.

The 1965 incident occurred on a flight from Los Angeles to San Francisco. I had arrived at the gate early because the shuttle flight had open seating, that is, no assigned seats, and I wanted to get a portside window seat. The reason involved my just-completed field work for my dissertation, an oceanographic study of a submarine canyon off the California coast. The canyon head is located between Santa Cruz and Santa Rosa Islands, two of the California Channel Islands some thirty or so miles offshore. The flight north to San Francisco would carry us just east of the two islands, and the rising sun (it was an early-morning flight) coupled with the cloudless blue sky promised an outstanding opportunity to photograph that area from a bird's-eye view.

I was the second person on board, and selected a first-row, portside window seat—just where I had wanted to be. The plane began to fill up, but the two seats beside me remained empty. A gentleman then walked aboard, looked around, and came over to me. He asked, very nicely, if I would mind selecting another seat, because there were two important passengers coming aboard who would want to occupy two seats in the front row. I indicated to him that there indeed were two seats available next to me in the front row, and his "important passengers" were certainly welcome to use those seats.

He then informed me that the passengers were the Secretary of Labor and his wife and that he was their press secretary and he would really appreciate a full front row, so they all could sit together. I looked around and saw no open window seats on the portside of the aircraft. He noted my hesitation, and exclaimed, politely, but firmly, "You don't seem to understand. This is the Secretary of Labor. He's a member of the President's cabinet, and he would very much want to occupy that seat."

Well, it *was* 1965. I *was* young. I still hadn't established residence in Washington, D.C. and so was impressed with an almost-royal title (Secretary of Labor—WOW!) It didn't even occur to me then that Mr. Secretary hadn't even paid for his own ticket, whereas I did. Anyway, I sheepishly left my seat and fumbled my way back to the—by then—only available open seat. It was on the aisle, midway aft, on the starboard side. Just before the front hatch closed, the Secretary and his wife made their appearance and the press secretary motioned them to their front row seats. As the plane took off I felt very foolish. I didn't feel any better when, ten minutes later, I caught a passing glimpse, an aisle and three seats away, of the Channel Islands.

The scene now shifts to 1990. Once again I'm in Los Angeles International Airport, having just boarded a flight to Pittsburgh. A sudden consulting opportunity had required a last-minute change in my itinerary, and instead of heading home I was off to Pittsburgh for two days. I had rushed to the airport and had been fortunate enough to be assigned the seat of a no-show. The aisle seat was soon occupied, and the middle seat remained empty. The flight, the only Pittsburgh nonstop of the day, filled up quickly, with even center seats disappearing as their unhappy occupants looked forward to five hours of sardine packaging. Listed departure time had come and gone, and as our center seat remained unoccupied it looked as if my aisle-mate and I would enjoy a comfortable trip back east.

But no such luck. Another passenger boarded the plane. She was dressed all in red, and her arrival coincided with the front hatch being secured. She came rumbling down the aisle clutching her boarding pass in one hand and an enormous duffel-like bag in the other. She stopped at our row, looked left and right, and with apparent dismay shook her head and announced, to nobody in particular, "No way I'm sitting in a center seat." She looked straight at me, dropped her carryon trunk, and barreling forward, she intercepted a flight attendant and dragged her back to our row. Grasping the flight attendant by her upper arm and glaring at me, she shouted, "That man is sitting in my seat. I want my seat. I am not going to sit in a center seat all the way home." Well, she *could* have been a Pittsburgh Steeler, but more likely a Pittsburgh Penguin. Hockey seemed to be more her style. I bet she was tough in the corners, and could cross-check with the best of them. Obviously I'd just met Ms. No-Show, and she blamed me for her late arrival at the gate and loss of her precious seat. When she received her new seat assignment, she apparently didn't realize it was a center seat.

The flight attendant, wriggling loose from the half-nelson, tried to calm her down, but to no avail. She repeated her demand for my (yes, *my*) seat. Finally, the attendant, whose people-training obviously included simulated passenger confrontations, leaned over and asked if I minded relinquishing my seat to the scarlet lady, whose facial coloration by now matched her clothes exactly.

It's funny, but I remember remembering, instantly, my encounter with the press secretary a quarter of a century earlier. Twenty-five years, and I still hadn't had another crack at taking an aerial photo of the Santa Cruz and Santa Rosa Islands. The attendant thought I wasn't listening, and she repeated her request to me to allow the Crimson Lady to acquire her original seat. If there is such a thing as body language, then the object of our discussion was daring me to refuse, as both her scowl and duffel were both threatening me with destruction. This time I smiled, and without rancor or hesitation said, "Yes, I do mind relinquishing my seat, I'm rather comfortable here." The melee moved aft, and I never knew if, where, or how the situation was settled. Perhaps they found a young graduate student who could be talked out of his window or aisle seat, and was now being squashed in a center seat somewhere in the airplane.

There always are and always will be those who are willing to take advantage of every opportunity to enhance their own position. And there always are and always will be those who are willing to assume a subservient role in any professional relationship. It's simply a question of which group you want to become part of. If you intend to work alone, remember, you may end up like me or like the lady in red. You see, I felt much closer to her, than I did to that submissive graduate student you met at the beginning of this tale.

When the plane took off, I pushed my seat back and dozed for a half-hour or so before pulling out some paper-work. It was a comfortable flight.

67 | SOARING

It's a good life

In a classic *60 Minutes* interview of pianist-comic Victor Borge, he was asked to compare his keyboard prowess to that of the great Vladimir Horowitz. Specifically, the question ended, " . . . Mr. Borge, what is the difference between you and Horowitz?" The implication was that, as entertaining as Borge's activities are, his comic stroking of the ivories was really far removed from Horowitz's genius. I felt it was a snobbish question, clearly meant to put Borge in his place, somewhere on the fringe of the classical music scene.

Mr. Borge, stone-faced as ever, paused a full three seconds, turned to the camera, and with a wicked twinkle in his eyes, said, "The difference is, he's dead." So much for classical genius. Instead then, of allowing himself to be placed in a position of defending his career choices, and launching into a long dissertation justifying his own life-style, Borge said simply, in essence, "Stuff it. I've done it my way, alone, and I've succeeded."

Working alone, you will come across many people, friends, relatives, past colleagues and the like, who really feel uncomfortable watching what you are doing. Many of these same people are permanently implanted neck deep in the mire of their own tightly bounded bantam worlds. They will see you pressing against the envelope of your knowledge. They will watch you moving from opportunity to opportunity while they remain trapped in the trauma of their own immobility. Often, they will claim, as you soar away from them, that it is *you* who are getting smaller and smaller. Believe me, they are wrong. Have a happy flight.

AN AFTERWORD
AND FINAL THOUGHT

Well. Now you know quite a bit about me and how I got to do the things I get to do. As I indicated in the "Introduction," I did not mean this to be a comprehensive manual on getting-into-a-money-making-business-on-your-own (though heaven knows, in these times that may not be such a bad idea for a next book). Instead, by specific and at times very personal example, I have attempted to create a philosophical template against which you can press your own past experiences and future expectations. I do not designate these essays as authoritative or as a final statement of any sort. Instead, they denote an always evolving mind-set; rigid enough to withstand the daily tumult facing any entrepreneur, yet flexible enough to respond to the expected denouements of circumstance and the whimsical consequences of chance.

This is a world where massive institutions are the vessels into which are poured the hopes and dreams of most individual workers. In such a world the mega-corporation, the mega-university, and the mega-government workplaces ostensibly serve to provide their work force with the security sought by the individual worker. In return for this measure of security, each worker is required to pay a heavy price, in terms of self-esteem, self-expression, and individual creativity. The vast majority of individuals, by far, is willing to sacrifice those special attributes in favor of a biweekly paycheck. Some few are not.

And in such a world, it takes a rather unusual, if not bold, and perhaps somewhat foolish person to place his trust within the ephemeral confines of his own self, as

opposed to the apparent permanence of a massive institutional entity. I am neither ashamed nor proud at being
called unusual, bold, and perhaps, somewhat foolish. I, and
those individuals who would rather work alone lead a rather
direct life, and we can claim immediate credit or immediate
blame for nearly everything that we do and that gets done to
us. It is a hands-on, no-buffer existence that, though it can
mix pain and pleasure, more often results in contentment
and fulfillment. Try it.

THE AUTHOR

Dr. Murray Felsher attended New York City public schools, including the Bronx High School of Science and C.C.N.Y. He received a Master of Science degree from the University of Massachusetts, his Ph.D. at the University of Texas at Austin, and then undertook postdoctoral research as a National Research Council of Canada Fellow at McMaster University before joining the geology department faculty at Syracuse University. In 1969 he left Syracuse University to run a two-year NSF-funded program at the American Geological Institute in Washington, D.C., intending to return to full-time teaching. Instead, he contracted "Potomac fever," and in 1971 joined the newly formed U.S. Environmental Protection Agency as the EPA headquarters' Office of Enforcement senior staff scientist. There he developed the agency's enforcement remote sensing program, and eventually was responsible for coordinating all of that agency's aircraft and space remote sensing activities as they related to EPA's national enforcement effort.

In 1975 Dr. Felsher transferred to NASA headquarters' Office of Applications and there served as Chief of the Geological and Energy Applications Program, Federal User Affairs Officer, Program Scientist for the Large Format Camera, Program Scientist for OSTA-1 (the first earth-viewing payload of the space shuttle), and originator (in 1976) of the National Space Grant College Program.

Dr. Felsher left government service in 1980 to form Associated Technical Consultants, a firm that has been providing technical and management consulting to the government and the private sector. In 1981 he began publishing *Washington Remote Sensing Letter*, now the oldest and most widely read commercial newsletter in its field. In 1989 he began publishing *Washington Federal Science Newsletter,* which reports on the science and technology programs of all federal departments and agencies. In 1993 volume 1, number 1 of *Defense Contract Awards* was published.